THE VANILLA BEAN BAKING BOOK

THE VANILLA BEAN BAKING BOOK

Recipes for Irresistible Everyday Favorites
and Reinvented Classics

SARAH KIEFFER

AVERY
an imprint of Penguin Random House
New York

AVERY

an imprint of Penguin Random House LLC
375 Hudson Street
New York, New York 10014

Most Avery books are available at special quantity discounts
for bulk purchase for sales promotions, premiums, fund-
raising, and educational needs. Special books or book
excerpts also can be created to fit specific needs. For details,
write SpecialMarkets@penguinrandomhouse.com.

Library of Congress Cataloging-in-Publication Data

Names: Kieffer, Sarah, author.
Title: The Vanilla Bean baking book : recipes for irresistible everyday
    favorites and reinvented classics / Sarah Kieffer.
Description: New York, New York : Avery, an imprint of Penguin Random House, LLC.
    [2016] | Recipes from the Vanilla Bean Blog.
Identifiers: LCCN 2016016459 | ISBN 9781583335840 (print) | ISBN 9780698198425 (ePub)
Subjects: LCSH: Desserts. | Cake. | LCGFT: Cookbooks.
Classification: LCC TX773. K488 2016 | DDC 642.86—dc23
LC record available at https://lccn.loc.gov/2016016459
p.   cm.

Printed in China
10 9 8 7 6 5 4 3 2 1

Book design by Jan Derevjanik

To Winter and River

Blossoms of snow may you bloom and grow,
bloom and grow forever.

CONTENTS

INTRODUCTION

Cookies were my gateway to baking. My kitchen adventures began with them, standing on a chair right next to my mom. Every winter holiday we spent days near the oven, my sister and I rolling out sugar cookie dough, decorating each cut-out tree, angel, and star. Our face and hands, along with our entire 1970s yellow tile floor would be coated in flour and Christmas-colored sprinkles. Fights between my sister and me would break out over cookie cutters, my little brother would crawl up on our chairs, begging to help, and my dad would pop in occasionally to steal cookie dough when our heads were turned. Most of the cookies would be passed out to neighbors later that week, the rest secretly snatched by our greedy little fingers.

It wasn't long before I started baking cookies on my own. I had such a thrill pulling down the worn-out church cookbook from the shelf above the stove and thumbing through it until I found our family's favorite chocolate chip cookie recipe. Many afternoons I would come home from school, take butter, sugar, eggs, and flour out from the cupboards, and get to work. I made just about every cookie and bar recipe in that old book, along with every recipe on the back of chocolate chip packages, flour bags, and oatmeal containers. I experimented with cookies made out of cake mix and cookies made with shortening. I started caring about how many crinkles the top of each confection had and perfected crisp edges and gooey centers. I baked them for my siblings, I took them to neighbors, and I brought them to my grandma. But I also made them for myself. Straight from the oven, those round, warm circles took away the heartache junior high brought. Stirring the cookie batter with my mom's old wooden spoon drove away the emotional discomfort, if only for a moment. I couldn't articulate it at the time, but I found contentment in both baking to keep and baking to give away.

I went to Winona State University after high school, determined to get an English degree and do something positive with it. Working part-time was a necessity, as my college career was on my own shoulders. With some barista experience under my belt, I applied at a small coffeehouse across from campus to help pay the bills. There, in that sleepy little river town nestled between the bluffs, cookie baking also became part of my college experience.

The cafe I worked for was the Blue Heron Coffeehouse, owned by Larry and Colleen Wolner. They had moved to Winona with their family to start their lifelong dream: bringing delicious, homemade food to the small-town community. The Blue Heron not only served coffee but made all their food and baked goods in-house. I started as their first and only employee and spent my weekday mornings and weekend evenings working the coffee bar. Business was slow at the beginning, but as it started to pick up, the demand for their baked goods did also. One day after a long shift, Larry asked me if I knew how to make cookies. I thought back to those afternoons at my parents' house, creaming butter and sugar with nothing but a wooden spoon and my own two hands. I assured him I did. He handed me their house chocolate chip cookie recipe, gave me specific instructions, and I set to work. I was out of practice and my first few batches didn't win any contests, but the Wolners were desperate, and I kept at it. A short week later I had found my groove and was baking off dozens of cookies I was proud of. Each shift, part of my routine became making a batch for the afternoon rush. Larry added oatmeal raisin to the list and peanut butter soon after. Before I knew it, I was making banana bread, coffee cakes, scones, muffins, and cheesecake as well. For almost five years I worked with Larry and Colleen, and never grew tired of my moments in the kitchen with them. I still made coffee every day for customers, but the stretches I got to head back to the prep table and bake were my favorite. Over my time there, they taught me essential kitchen skills like how to knead bread, cut butter into flour, and how to frost a cake. They taught me to care about where my ingredients came from and to use quality products in my baked goods and cooking. They taught me that my state of mind mattered and entering work happy, sad, or frustrated could affect how my final product would turn out. When I graduated, I headed home with my English degree, but I now understand my real education had been happening in the kitchen of the Blue Heron.

After college I did what many English majors do; I worked as a bookseller and barista for a few years, wondering what to do with my life. Eventually, however, I found my way back into the kitchen. A friend had started a small coffeehouse, Bordertown Coffee, in an old fraternity house that he renovated, and I was given the smallest area imaginable to bake in. My space consisted of a stainless square prep table, two tiny convection ovens, and a kitchen sink for washing dishes. Not only was I in charge of that tiny kitchen but I was also the only person working in it. Fifty to sixty hours a week I was there before dawn, baking scones, muffins, cookies, bars, tarts, pies,

cupcakes, and cakes; my time divided between baking like crazy and washing piles of dishes. There was no one to hold my hand in this space, to guide me through recipes when I had questions, and I was equally excited and terrified at running the kitchen myself. I made plenty of mistakes, but discovered that each one brought an important lesson, either in baking or in life. As our little coffeehouse became busier each day and the baristas were frequently engaged with customers, I found myself constantly alone, with only myself to talk to. It was there, in that box of a room hunched over my prep table, that I discovered layers to baking. I had an almost metaphysical response to baking; I loved all the movements involved, and creating something beautiful with my hands every day was pure delight. But there was an emotional need to baking as well. The stir of the spatula or the whisk, each turn of the dough brought total contentment. Every time a customer bought a warm scone and her face lit up, there was also a reward for me. I watched person after person find comfort in our tiny little shop, eating the baked goods I had worked so hard to make. Often it was just a short moment: someone biting into a piece of pound cake, or giving a sigh of satisfaction at an afternoon cookie break, but those flickers of joy made my 5 A.M. wake-up call manageable; made the achy legs, the sore back, the heavy lifting, the washing dishes, and the long hours bearable. And not just bearable, but satisfying. It gave me something intangibly wonderful that I never found on my academic journey.

I discovered other memories, too. Making a pie reminded me of Grandma Ethel; her towering frame in the kitchen, her long fingers delicately rolling out dough. Baking scones took me back to the Blue Heron, with pots of soup simmering on the stovetop, and Colleen humming along to Joni Mitchell on the stereo. Each cookie I decorated reminded me of my sister, still in her purple nightgown, baking with me on Christmas Eve. A cup full of chocolate chips stirred up an adolescent reflection of walking down the corridor and desperately trying to conjure up an invisibility cloak. Most impressions were beautiful; others, bittersweet. Some brought sheer pain. I was grateful for the time there to bake myself through them all. As I whisked and stirred, the people connected to those recipes and materials were there with me, crammed into that space. I discovered I was never really alone.

I took my own secret fire I had cultivated with me after I left my kitchen in the fraternity house. I am married now, with two small children, baking and writing from home. It has been a place for all of us to continue learning about the layers of life and a space to create new memories together. As I bake with my children, I walk them through recipes and teach them technique, but I also tell them stories from my past. I tell them of my many mistakes, of how it took me years to be disciplined and follow a recipe as written the first time through. I tell them about my grandmothers and how one loved to bake and the other did not. I tell them about when my siblings and I would battle over sprinkles and the time I made the worst rhubarb crisp ever. I tell them about when I baked an apple pie for the first time, in the apartment where I began my married life. The kitchens from the past intertwine in our own current space, and as my little ones stand on chairs next to me, coated in flour and fighting over cookies cutters, I know they will have this moment, this story, in kitchens to come.

"It seems to me that our three basic needs, for food and security and love, are so mixed and mingled and entwined that we cannot straightly think of one without the others. So it happens that when I write of hunger, I am really writing about love and the hunger for it, and warmth and the love of it and the hunger for it . . . and then the warmth and richness and fine reality of hunger satisfied . . . and it is all one." —M.F.K. FISHER

ABOUT *THE VANILLA BEAN BLOG*

I started *The Vanilla Bean Blog* in 2011 as a space devoted to recipes, photographs, and occasional musings and reflections. It was an attempt to document a food history of sorts for my family; we had none, and I wanted to change that. In the process I discovered many overlays to my time in the kitchen. I have always found comfort in the act of baking, and while I enjoy the end result of a kitchen filled with sweet treats, I find there is so much more to it than just sugar and butter, some flour and eggs.

There is such value to *what we are actually making*. The dishes and meals we make for loved ones and the act of preparing them: to cook and bake and eat them together connects us beyond the physical. It's not about eating or creating just for the sake of doing so. There is something deeper, something *soul*-full that happens when we slice the cake, when we break the bread. There is taste and smell that draws out memories, binding us to those present, those past. There is purpose in our food: both the physical and the unconscious, the labor of our hands, the labor of our heart. This, to me, is real communion: the act of sharing, the act of receiving.

How to Use This Book

While I have worked professionally in several coffeehouses, I am, first and foremost, a home baker and have written this book with the home baker and home kitchen in mind. Any knowledge I have about baking comes from watching others, reading piles of books, and making something again and again until it is how I want it. While I respect the expertise and dedication of pastry chefs everywhere, there is room in the universe for creativity and artistry at home.

There are many recipes requiring varying skills throughout these pages; some are easy and some demand a bit more time and patience. Be sure to follow the baking tips on pages 17–20, and read through the ingredient and equipment lists, also in this chapter, for helpful advice and reference. When writing the directions for the recipes, I assumed you have some baking experience and know your way around the kitchen enough to make a batch of cookies or a cake from scratch. However, if a recipe here seems out of your comfort zone, I encourage you to try it, even if it seems intimidating. The worst that can happen is it won't turn out exactly right, and you'll be able to make it again with a new experience under your belt.

This book is divided into seven chapters, each with a different focus. "Morning Baking" starts things off and includes both yeasted and non-yeasted items, everything from granola to scones to Easy Danish Dough (page 71). "Quick Breads, Muffins, and

Everyday Cakes" is next, and you'll discover sweets that require a bit less work. Banana Bread (page 90), Blueberry Muffins (page 85), and Picnic Cakes (page 114) are found here. I'll also allude to J. R. R. Tolkien's Middle-earth one too many times in that chapter, but it can't be helped. A variety of layer cakes grace the "Party Cakes" chapter. I'll walk you through baking and frosting cakes, plus various types of buttercream and cake bases. Cheesecakes also make an appearance. "Pies and Tarts" are fourth on the list, and I'll tell you about my pie-making trials, share my favorite All-Butter Pie Crust (page 187), and turn you on to Pear-Chocolate Galettes (page 219) and Cherry-Rhubarb Crisp with White Wine (page 217). "Cookies and Bars" follows, with my totally revamped Chocolate Chip Cookies recipe (page 237) starting things off. Don't skip the Oatmeal Cookies with White Chocolate and Golden Raisins (page 242) and the Coffee Blondies (page 258), an all-time favorite. "No-Churn Ice Cream" is the rogue chapter, but the flavors work well with many of the other recipes included here. And finally, "Homemade Staples" closes the book, with recipes for Crème Fraîche (page 305), Chocolate Ganache (page 309), and Caramel Sauce (page 316), among others.

A Few Other Things to Note

A PINCH SALT is often called for throughout the book. It is a little more than ⅛ teaspoon, but less than ¼ teaspoon.

Scant means just a little bit under the measurement; *heaping* means a little bit more than the measurement.

TO MAKE AN EGG WASH · Use a fork to whisk 1 large egg, a pinch of salt, and 1 tablespoon of water together in a small bowl. Use to brush on pie crusts, tart shells, and so on.

MEASURING FLOUR · Throughout this book, 1 cup of flour is equal to 5 ounces or 142 grams. This measurement is on the higher end of the scale (1 cup of flour usually ranges from 4 to 5 ounces, depending on the baker), but I found after weighing many cups of flour and averaging the total, mine usually came out to be 4.9 ounces, and I rounded up for convenience. I later made the decision to record ingredient measurements in both cups and grams and not include ounces, but if you prefer to weigh your ingredients in ounces, there is a conversion chart at the back of the book.

MEASURING SEMISOLIDS · Sour cream, peanut butter, pumpkin puree, and yogurt are all examples of semisolid ingredients, falling somewhere between a liquid and a solid.

There is much debate on the proper way to measure them, with the most accurate way being to weigh them. I was always taught to measure these wetter ingredients in liquid measuring cups, and so I always have. When testing recipes for the book, I discovered that a liquid measuring cup gave me a little more volume than a dry measuring cup. For instance, 1 cup sour cream in a dry measure weighed 8.4 ounces, but in a liquid measure, it weighed 9.1 ounces. This isn't a huge difference, but I felt it was slightly noticeable in some recipes. Because this cookbook lists the measurements for semisolid ingredients in cups and not grams, I recommend using a liquid measuring cup for them.

LINING PANS AND LOAF PANS WITH PARCHMENT PAPER · Lining pans and loaf pans with a parchment sling results in an easy release. Cut two pieces of parchment paper the same size as the bottom of your pan and long enough to come up and over the sides. Spray the pan with cooking spray and then place the pieces of parchment in the pan, perpendicular to each other, making sure to push the sheets into the corners.

LINING A CAKE PAN · Cut circles of parchment paper the same size as the bottom of your cake pan. Use a generous amount of room temperature butter to grease the sides and bottom of the pan, coating them with a thin, even layer of butter that covers the entire inside surface. Place the parchment circle in the bottom of the pan. Coat the paper with a thin, even layer of butter as well. Place 2 to 3 tablespoons of flour in the cake pan and move the pan around, distributing the flour so it evenly coats the butter. (I find turning the pan on its side and moving it in a circle works to get the sides.) When the butter is coated, gently tap the pan upside down over your sink to remove any excess flour.

BAKING TIPS

Read the Recipe and Then Follow the Recipe

It is very important to read the entire recipe thoroughly before starting to bake. I have made the mistake so many times of skimming half a recipe and then jumping in, only to discover I didn't have an ingredient I needed, or the recipe process took much longer than I expected it to. Make sure to read the entire recipe once, even twice before beginning. After you feel confident making a recipe there is always room to personalize it.

Mise en Place

Mise en place is a French phrase that literally means "put in place." This is a practice many chefs partake in—having all things ready before cooking or baking begins. This includes everything from ingredients prepped to equipment greased and lined to a preheated oven. It helps ensure the recipe will be executed in a fluid motion, without interruption.

At its core, mise en place is a way of life. It is a ritual meant to focus and connect you to the present, to what your hands are doing in the moment, without disturbance or distraction. Having everything in order will give you more of an opportunity to succeed in your task without wasting resources, including time and space. This practice may be difficult to fully embrace at first, but anyone who spends time in the kitchen learns that rushing steps or not looking ahead can result in sunken cakes, burned chocolate, and overcooked egg whites. Take a few extra moments in the beginning to do things well and you are more likely to see a good outcome.

Use Your Senses

As the author of this book, I am here to guide you as best as I can through each of these recipes. However, my oven, equipment, weather, and state of mind can and will be different from yours. If your oven isn't calibrated to the right temperature, your baked goods will probably not turn out as described (see oven thermometer, page 30). High altitude and humidity can affect baking. Feeling depressed or anxious can influence your concentration and, therefore, could possibly alter how you read a recipe. Because I am not there with you to guide you should any of these things occur, you need to rely on your senses. If you open the oven and the cake looks like it is browning too quickly, check to see if it should come out. If the pumpkin bread is still doughy in the middle even though the baking time has elapsed, keep it in the oven longer. Using your eyes and nose will help you recognize when your baked goods are done. Your palate and hands are also good tools.

A Nod to the Food Gods

When I worked at the Blue Heron, I spent a lot of time making banana bread. It was one of my daily tasks, and after years of mixing and mashing I could have made the bread in my sleep. However, one Friday afternoon, after making it had become more routine than pleasure, I baked four loaves that sunk in the middle and tasted terrible. Larry walked over to my prep table to take a peek at the wasted loaves, and I'll never forget his words: "The kitchen gods are always watching," he said. "You may think you have a recipe down, but the minute you feel you own a recipe or lack humbleness for your ingredients and movements, the gods will remind you, and teach you respect again." His sincerity etched those sentences in my mind, and I recall them each time I am in the kitchen.

I'm not going to try to convince you that Hestia, the goddess of the hearth, is there in your kitchen, waiting to strike you at every false move. However, I think there is truth in the notion that how we approach our work affects how it turns out. There are many variables to this, but I've always found that when I am overconfident or assume that what I make will turn out perfectly, I often am unconsciously careless and make a mistake. I've learned to approach my kitchen counter with both humility and confidence, trepidation mixed with reverence.

Learn from Your Mistakes

Every dry cake, doughy quick bread, scorched caramel, and over-whipped cream is a chance to learn something. When all goes wrong, recall the steps of the recipe and figure out where you made your mistake. Make a note of it, in a baking journal or right in the cookbook, so you don't make the same mistake twice. Don't be afraid of baking mishaps, but use them as an opportunity to grow and learn. As Julia Child said, *"Eh bien, tant pis!"*

Be a Lifelong Learner

While I often dream of moving to France for a year or two and attending pastry school, that isn't something I can make a reality at this point in my life, or probably ever. I have two small children and roots planted firmly in Minneapolis. But even so, and even despite the fact that I've baked professionally over the years, I know I can always learn more and hone my craft. Here are some things that have helped me:

THE LIBRARY · The library has access to every possible baking book you can imagine. Go to your local library, or search online for subjects that interest you, and then check out books and bake from them. You can later purchase the books you discover you can't live without.

BAKING CLASSES · Often local cooking stores and even co-ops and grocery stores offer baking and cooking classes. They sometimes even feature national and local chefs and hands-on demonstrations. I've taken several classes over the years and have learned so much by listening to others talk about their experiences.

START A BAKING GROUP · Get a group of friends or locals together to bake or just chat about baking. Pick a new dessert to make each time or have everyone make a different recipe at home to share and then talk about how the recipe worked or didn't work and what he or she learned.

If you really want to learn a craft, you have to be willing to invest time into it. Baking can be just a fun pastime, but if you want it to be more than that, there are ways to learn and practice without moving to a different continent. Don't be afraid to try.

INGREDIENTS

The following is a list of ingredients used in the book, ones I always have on hand in my own kitchen pantry. As someone who bakes often, both for business and pleasure, I find I use most of these ingredients on a regular basis. Many of these should be easy for you to find in your local grocery store; for the few ingredients that are specialty items or are hard to find, see the "Resources" section at the back of the book. Remember when choosing ingredients that high-quality items will yield better results. When I begin to test a recipe or when I am baking something for the first time, I use cheaper ingredients until I get the end product just how I want it. Then I test the recipe one final time with high-quality butter, chocolate, honey, and so on and find the result to be a much better version of whatever I have been making.

Dairy + Eggs

BUTTER · All the recipes in this book call for unsalted butter. Using unsalted butter helps regulate how much salt is actually used. If you decide to use salted butter anyway, you will want to use a little less salt overall. A European-style butter (a butter with more fat content) also works wonderfully in many applications, but please note that it isn't always a good swap in all recipes. For instance, the high fat content can cause extra spreading in cookies. Land O'Lakes unsalted (sweet) butter is a good choice and the best grocery store option for recipes. I do not suggest substituting oils for butter.

MILK · All recipes in this book were tested with whole milk. I don't recommend replacing whole milk with skim milk; there is much less fat in skim milk and this can impact the outcome of the recipe.

HEAVY CREAM · Heavy cream is also known as double cream. Look for one that is pasteurized, not ultra-pasteurized when making crème fraîche.

BUTTERMILK · There are quite a few recipes that call for buttermilk in this book. If you do not have any on hand, you can make some in a pinch. For every cup of milk you need, add 1 tablespoon lemon juice or vinegar to it. Whisk the milk and vinegar together and let it sit for 10 minutes at room temperature. The milk is ready when it starts to thicken. It will not be quite as thick and creamy as store-bought buttermilk but will still work just fine in the recipe.

CREAM CHEESE · Any grocery store cream cheese will work in these recipes. I've found Philadelphia brand cream cheese to taste the best overall, and it is the only kind I'll use in my cheesecakes.

EGGS · All recipes in this book call for Grade A large eggs. A large egg, in its shell, should weigh 2 ounces (57 grams). Personally, I prefer to bake with local, farm-fresh eggs. I've found them to consistently have beautiful orange yolks. However, store-bought eggs will also work fine in all these recipes. Some recipes call for room temperature eggs. If you need to bring the eggs to room temperature quickly, place the eggs in a large bowl, and cover them with warm water. Let them sit for 10 minutes. If you need to separate the egg whites and the yolk, generally it's easier to start with a cold egg because the yolk will be firmer. After the egg is separated, let the yolks and whites come to room temperature if the recipe calls for it. If you find you have leftover egg yolks, place them in a small bowl, cover them completely with water, and store in the fridge for up to 3 days. Drain the water before using. Leftover egg whites can be placed in a small bowl, covered with plastic wrap, and stored in the fridge for 3 days. You can also freeze egg whites. Place the whites in a tightly sealed container and freeze for up to a year.

Cooking Oils

CANOLA OIL · Canola oil is a neutral-flavored oil and is the most common oil you'll find called for in this book.

OLIVE OIL · Certain recipes in this book really require good-quality extra-virgin olive oil. I'll make a note in the recipe for you when a better brand is needed. Terra Medi extra-virgin olive oil and Lucini extra-virgin olive oil are two store-bought brands I use frequently.

TOASTED SESAME OIL · Toasted sesame oil is mostly used in savory preparations, but I've found pairing it with sugar is absolutely delicious (see Chocolate Chip Cookies on page 237 and Caramel Sauce on page 316). La Tourangelle makes a higher end grocery store toasted sesame oil, which I use in small amounts in baking.

Salt + Spices

TABLE SALT · All recipes in this cookbook use table salt, unless otherwise noted. Table salt is much finer than kosher or sea salts and dissolves more quickly when baked.

FLEUR DE SEL (flower of salt, in French) · A fine, delicate, moist salt that's used as a finishing salt. Because of its high moisture content, the salt crystals stick together when gathered and don't dissolve right away when eaten. This means the salt takes longer to melt in your mouth and that salty taste lingers just a bit longer than regular salt. Coarse sea salt can be substituted.

SPICES · Spices have a shelf life and can grow stale or rancid over time. Make sure your spices have not been sitting for years in the cupboard before using them; it's a good idea to update them every year. While I use many preground spices in my baking, for nutmeg I prefer to grate it fresh myself.

Sweeteners

SUGAR · All recipes in this book were tested with regular granulated sugar. Organic granulated sugar can be substituted in many recipes, but please note that most organic sugar has a coarser grain than regular white sugar, which means it may not melt as quickly as finer-ground sugar. This can cause problems in some recipes. If you prefer organic sugar, you can process it in a food processor until it is finely ground before using.

BROWN SUGAR · Recipes in this book call for brown sugar and were tested with light brown sugar. Dark brown sugar can be substituted with good results.

CONFECTIONERS' SUGAR · Powdered sugar is also known as confectioners' sugar and icing sugar.

CORN SYRUP · Light corn syrup is called for occasionally throughout the book, as it gives a glossy, smooth texture in some buttercreams. Do not substitute dark corn syrup for light. Dark corn syrup has a more robust flavor and is not a good replacement in these recipes.

TURBINADO SUGAR · Turbinado sugar is a sugar that is minimally refined. It is light brown in color and has larger crystals than granulated sugar. It is used often on the tops of baked goods to give a little crunch and sparkle.

Flour

ALL-PURPOSE · All the recipes in this book were tested with unbleached all-purpose flour. To measure flour, I highly recommend using a digital scale (see page 27) and have provided weight measurements accordingly. To measure flour without a scale, I use the dip-and-sweep method: Dip the measuring cup into the bag or container of flour. Pull the cup out, with the flour overfilling the cup. Sweep the excess off the top with a knife, so that you have a level cup of flour.

Leavenings

BAKING POWDER · I prefer to bake with non-aluminum baking powder. Brands with aluminum can give off the taste of metal, especially in recipes that use a lot of it, like biscuits and scones. Rumford sells an aluminum-free grocery store option. While baking soda seems to never expire, baking powder has a lifespan of about 6 months. If you are unsure if your baking powder is still potent, add a spoonful of it to a cup of hot water. If it bubbles, it's still good to use.

BAKING SODA · Baking soda needs to be paired with an acidic ingredient in order to be activated to help baked goods rise. Buttermilk, sour cream, yogurt, and vinegar are commonly used acidic ingredients, but coffee, molasses, brown sugar, and pumpkin are a few others.

YEAST · I use instant yeast (also called rapid-rise yeast) in all recipes calling for yeast. Instant yeast does not need to be proofed and can be added directly to the dry ingredients.

Nuts

Certain recipes in this book call for pistachios and toasted pecans. Because nuts can turn rancid very quickly, I like to toast nuts as soon as I purchase them and store them in the freezer. To toast nuts, place an oven rack in the middle position and preheat the oven to 350°F. Line a baking sheet with parchment paper and place the nuts in the prepared pan in a single layer. Bake 5 to 10 minutes (time depends on the size of the nuts), until they darken and are fragrant (I like my pecans very dark and toast them a bit longer). Let the nuts cool and store them in a self-sealing plastic bag in the freezer.

Chocolate

BITTERSWEET/SEMISWEET BAR CHOCOLATE · *Bittersweet* and *semisweet* are not really helpful terms, as both can mean chocolate with a cacao percentage of anywhere from 35 to 99 percent (although most stay in the 35 to 60 percent range). Many of the recipes here call for bittersweet chocolate, in bar form. Look for a chocolate baking bar with 60 percent or less cacao and don't use anything 70 percent or over, as this can alter the taste and texture of the recipe. A good supermarket brand is Ghirardelli bittersweet chocolate (60 percent cacao) or Ghirardelli semisweet chocolate.

When melting chocolate, it helps to chop the bar into small pieces. The chocolate will melt more quickly and evenly and will have less opportunity to burn. Make sure when you are melting chocolate that there is no water (not even a drop!) in your bowl, or on your knife or spatula. Contact with water can cause the chocolate to seize, turning it into a grainy paste. Adding a tablespoon or two of hot water to the seized chocolate and then stirring it can sometimes save it.

To melt chocolate, either use a double boiler or melt the chocolate in the microwave. If melting the chocolate in the microwave, place the chopped chocolate in a microwave-safe bowl (I like to use a glass Pyrex measuring cup). Microwave the chocolate on medium for 1 minute, then stop and stir the chocolate. Continue to microwave the chocolate for 20-second intervals, stopping to stir after each one, until the chocolate is almost completely smooth. Remove the container from the microwave and stir until the chocolate is completely smooth.

CHOCOLATE CHIPS · I use Ghirardelli 60 percent cacao bittersweet chocolate chips, or Guittard real semisweet chocolate chips. Chocolate chips have less cacao than bar chocolate, which allows them to hold their shape when melted. This means they are not a good substitution for bar chocolate; they will not melt as quickly or as smoothly. Have I, in a pinch, used chocolate chips for bar chocolate? Yes. Have I regretted it? About half the time.

WHITE CHOCOLATE · Some chocolate purists say that white chocolate isn't real chocolate, but it is made from cocoa butter, so I say it counts. It is important to note that white chocolate melts much more quickly than dark chocolate. Be sure to stir it more frequently than you would dark chocolate, especially when using the microwave. It will turn thick and burn if overcooked. White chocolate chips do not melt well at all; I prefer to use white bar chocolate. Callebaut is an expensive but delicious white chocolate option. Ghirardelli makes a fine grocery store option as well.

COCOA POWDER · Cocoa powder is chocolate liquor with a good majority of the cacao butter removed from it. What remains is then turned into powder form. There are two kinds of cocoa powder: natural and Dutch process. Natural cocoa powder is left as is—a very acidic, sharp powder. Dutch process cocoa is treated; it is washed with an alkaline solution that neutralizes its acids and has a more mellow, nutty flavor and a richer color.

Because one cocoa powder is acidic and the other is not, this means a recipe can be affected quite a bit by using the wrong type of cocoa powder. There are many variables involved, so it's best to go with the cocoa powder the recipe author calls for. If it isn't clear, there is a simple rule that should work most of the time: Dutch process works best when the recipe also calls for baking powder (a neutral pH) and natural cocoa powder works best when the recipe calls for baking soda (an alkaline). If a recipe calls for both baking soda and baking powder, you can use either type of cocoa powder as long as there is a larger amount of baking powder than soda. You can also use both types of cocoa powder if baking soda is used with another acidic ingredient (buttermilk, sour cream, and so on). A Dutch process cocoa powder works in all of the recipes in this book unless noted. Hershey's Special Dark cocoa, which is a blend of both natural and Dutch process cocoas, is a good grocery store option, and also works in all of the recipes found here. Valrhona cocoa powder is a more expensive option, one I save for special occasions.

CACAO NIBS · Cacao nibs are essentially the bare bones of chocolate; they come straight from the cocoa tree. Cocoa beans are roasted, cracked, and deshelled and the broken pieces are called nibs. Nibs are either used as is or are ground into a paste, also known as chocolate liquor. The nibs themselves have a complex, bitter flavor and are crunchy to eat.

Vanilla

VANILLA EXTRACT · All the recipes in this book use pure vanilla extract; I don't recommend using artificial vanilla. I prefer to make my own extract (see page 307).

VANILLA BEANS · Vanilla beans add a delicious flavor to baked goods and come in many varieties. Bourbon and Madagascar are great choices. To use a vanilla bean: use a sharp knife to split the bean lengthwise and then scrape the seeds out of the bean with the knife or a spoon. Use the collected beans in the recipe as called for. The leftover pod can be dried and then ground fine in a food processor, and small amounts of it can be used to give a subtle vanilla flavor to baked goods.

Coffee

As a huge fan of coffee, I like to bake with it quite often. You will find it accented in a few recipes throughout the book and often paired with chocolate. Coffee brings out the intense flavor of chocolate, and I use it in cakes and brownies to help the chocolate shine. It can be omitted in these recipes, but I highly recommend using it.

Different coffee beans will bring out different flavors when baking with them. When I am using coffee for the sole purpose of baking, I brew a non-acidic dark roast; I like the smooth, rich flavor it lends. Use the coffee at the temperature the recipe calls for (usually described as fresh brewed and hot, room temperature, or cold). I also brew a large pot of coffee and chill it; I keep it in a glass container in the refrigerator. Since I bake with coffee quite a bit, this means I always have coffee ready to use. If the recipe calls for it cold, I don't have to wait for it to chill, and if it needs to be hot, I can gently heat it on the stovetop or in the microwave.

EQUIPMENT

Measuring Equipment

DIGITAL SCALE · It is important to measure correctly, so that what you are making will turn out as it should. A digital scale will ensure the correct amounts of ingredients when you bake. Throughout this book I have weights listed for many ingredients: flour, sugars, butter, cocoa powder, chocolate, and the like. I have not included smaller measurements that can be measured in tablespoons or teaspoons. A digital kitchen scale is a very helpful tool; I use it not only for measuring flour but also for portioning out cookie dough, biscuits, and equally dividing cake batter between pans.

MEASURING CUPS AND SPOONS · Dry measuring cups are used to measure dry ingredients, such as flour, sugars, and cocoa powder. I use metal cups that come in different sizes: ¼, ⅓, ½, and 1 cup. I use metal measuring spoons for teaspoon and tablespoon measures; these come in sizes ¼, ½, and 1 teaspoon, and 1 tablespoon. For liquids I use glass measuring cups with a pourable spout, and which have measurements marked along the side of the cup.

Utensils

WIRE WHISK · I use whisks for many kitchen tasks: beating eggs, mixing batter, combining dry ingredients, and smoothing ganache.

SILICONE SPATULAS · Spatulas are an essential kitchen tool. They have so many uses: folding, smoothing, stirring, mixing, and scraping down sides, just to name a few. I have several spatulas, all in different sizes, and use them daily.

OFFSET SPATULA · Offset spatulas are used for icing cakes and spreading batter evenly into pans. I have a small and a large one and prefer them with a rounded edge verses a straight edge.

ZESTER · A microplane zester comes in handy when a recipe calls for the zest of an orange or lemon or freshly grated nutmeg or gingerroot.

ROLLING PIN · I prefer a wood pin when rolling out doughs and usually use a French rolling pin, which is a handle-free straight rolling pin; some of them are tapered at the ends.

SERRATED BREAD KNIFE · A good serrated knife is a great tool for cutting cake layers in half and slicing finished cakes.

SKEWERS · I use wooden skewers for testing cakes, muffins, quick breads, and the like. A toothpick can also be used.

PASTRY BRUSHES · Over the years, pastry brushes have become essential to my kitchen. I use them for glazing scones with heavy cream, coating pies with egg wash, and brushing away crumbs. I use a natural-bristle brush; I've found them to work much better than silicone, although they need to be replaced more frequently.

RULER · I highly recommend having a ruler in your kitchen. It comes in useful for measuring the length and width of dough that needs to be rolled out or sliced. I have an 18-inch-long ruler that works perfectly.

BENCH SCRAPER · A bench scraper has many purposes, from transferring ingredients, to lifting doughs off the counter, cutting doughs, and cleaning the work surface.

KITCHEN SCISSORS · Kitchen scissors are a very useful tool with many functions, like cutting parchment paper, pastry bag tips, and cardboard rounds as well as snipping dough.

PASTRY CUTTER · I use pastry cutters all the time for things like trimming rolled doughs and making lattice crusts. A pizza cutter will also work for these applications.

PASTRY BLENDER · When making scones and pie crust by hand, a pastry blender is ideal for cutting the butter into the flour.

HEAVY-DUTY STAND MIXER · Many of the recipes in this book use a stand mixer, although often a hand-held mixer or a sturdy spoon can be substituted. If you do a lot of baking, I highly recommend investing in a stand mixer for both convenience and speed.

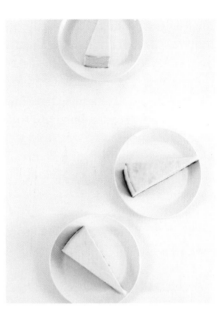

FOOD PROCESSOR · I find a food processor very handy in the kitchen, although I don't use it as much as other equipment. I make galette dough in the food processor and also use it for pulverizing nuts, grating carrots quickly, and occasionally making pizza dough.

MIXING BOWLS · I mostly use glass mixing bowls of various sizes in my kitchen, although I do have a few stainless steel bowls as well. A large, deep bowl is a good idea to have around, for mixing muffin batter, cutting butter into flour, and stirring brownie batter.

PARCHMENT PAPER · Parchment paper is excellent for lining cake pans, loaf pans, and baking sheets. It makes for an easy cleanup, and baked goods come out of their vessels much easier. I like to buy my parchment paper from a restaurant supply store, where the sheets come precut and lay flat; I find them a bit easier to work with.

BAKING DISHES AND PANS (FOR LOAVES, CAKES, BROWNIES, AND MUFFINS) · I usually choose a medium-weight, light-colored aluminum pan (thin, darker pans can cause overbrowning in many cases) for all my cakes and loaves. I never use glass pans for baking cakes, bars, or brownies, as these pans tend to overbake the edges.

Most quick bread recipes in this book can be made in an 8- or 9-inch loaf pan. I prefer an 8-inch pan because the bread bakes up a bit taller with straighter sides, which

I find more attractive. My recipe times are based on an 8-inch pan. If you use a 9-inch pan, you will need to take a few minutes off the baking time.

PULLMAN PAN · Pullman pans are long, narrow pans with a lid. They are typically used for sandwich bread—the dough rises inside the lidded pan and, when baked, creates a square-shaped loaf. I've found that without the lid, they are excellent pans for baking quick bread. The longer, thin shape of the pan makes for an elegant-looking loaf, and the taller sides ensure that the batter won't spill over into the oven. I've found this pan to be especially useful when making Chocolate Bread (page 93). My pan is 9 by 4 by 4 inches.

BAKING SHEET · I use only medium-weight half sheet pans (12 by 16 inches, with a 1-inch rim), unless noted. I've found these pans work best for baking evenly in the oven.

PIE PLATE/PAN · I almost exclusively use a glass pie plate when baking pies. I like how the glass browns the crust, and I can also see through the pan, to check on how the bottom of the crust is baking. It is also nonreactive. A metal pie plate comes in second place; it also browns well. I use a 9 by 1-inch pan for all my pies, unless noted.

TART PAN · Removable-bottom tart pans come in many different sizes and finishes. I prefer a tinned steel pan to a darker pan or even a nonstick pan. I have a 9-inch pan and a 10-inch pan.

SPRINGFORM PAN · I use springform pans for cheesecakes and occasionally for coffee cakes. I have found that a springform pan with silicone sides works well; it easily releases the cheesecake and keeps the sides smooth. Lekue makes a silicone-sided pan with a white ceramic bottom that works well for serving, and you don't have to worry about trying to get the cheesecake off the metal bottom to a separate serving plate.

WIRE COOLING RACK · Cooling racks help speed up cooling times and help the bottom of baked goods stay crisp.

OVEN THERMOMETER · It is a good idea to keep an oven thermometer in your oven. Many ovens are not properly calibrated, and a wrong oven temperature can greatly affect the outcome of your baked goods. I have an inexpensive oven thermometer that I keep hanging on the middle rack of my oven, so I can constantly keep an eye on the temperature inside.

PORTION SCOOP · Portion scoops are nice to have, but not essential. I use them for scooping cookies, muffin batter, and ice cream and have them in a variety of sizes. Vollrath makes a reliable scoop that doesn't break easily.

CAKE DECORATING TURNTABLE · For years I declared that turntables were not necessary to frosting cakes. After buying one, I realized how much easier they make the frosting process. If you make a lot of cakes, a turntable is a good investment. I have the Ateco #612 revolving cake stand.

CARDBOARD CAKE ROUNDS · A cardboard round fits perfectly under cake layers and helps make transporting cakes from a turntable to a serving plate or cake carrier an easier job.

PASTRY BAGS WITH TIPS · I use large pastry bags for decorating cakes, or piping whipped cream or meringue. I have a handful of tips that I use for decorating and cleaning up cake edges. A few tips that I have in my collection are several sizes of plain tips, an open star tip (Ateco #823), a closed star tip (Ateco #848), and a leaf tip (Ateco #70).

ICING COMB · Although an icing comb is a nonessential piece of equipment, it is a nice tool to have for decorating cakes. It looks like a large comb and is used to create lines and patterns on the sides of a cake.

DOUBLE BOILER · A double boiler is a combo of two pots: a large one and a smaller one that sits on top. It's used for cooking ingredients that may have a tendency to seize or separate over direct heat, like chocolate, for example. You want to fill the bottom pan with an inch of water and set the smaller pan on top. The water in the bottom pan will begin to simmer as it's heated and will provide a gentle, steady heat to the pan above. You can make your own double boiler if needed. Set a mixing bowl over a saucepan of simmering water. Make sure the bottom of the mixing bowl doesn't touch the surface of the water, and it will work just like a store-bought double boiler.

MICROWAVE OVEN · I find I use my microwave quite a bit when baking. It is useful alternative to a double boiler for melting butter and chocolate and also works well to heat milk.

KITCHEN TORCH · A kitchen torch is another nonessential, but it's a tool I absolutely love. I use my kitchen torch to brown meringue and caramelize sugar, but it can be used for a variety of other tasks, such as broiling grapefruit, toasting marshmallows, and melting cheese.

chapter one

MORNING BAKING

Mornings are my favorite time to be in the kitchen. Most of my full-time baking career was Monday through Friday on the 5 A.M. shift, and while I dreaded that alarm clock going off before the sun was even up, once I was in the kitchen, I felt downright happy. I usually started the day by putting on Ella Fitzgerald, trying to scat along with her while mixing batter and cutting butter into flour. I discovered many things during those early hours, including the fact that eating scones in the first 20 minutes they are out of the oven is the best time to partake of them, and many, many customers felt it was acceptable to eat warm chocolate chip cookies for breakfast every single day. I can't say I blame them.

My favorite recipes in this chapter are the Pumpkin Scones and Cinnamon Rolls. I make both frequently in my home. The scones can be made the morning you need them, while the cinnamon rolls require some day-before prep time. Both are a perfect choice for a large breakfast gathering, or nibbling alone in the quiet morning hours.

PEANUT BUTTER GRANOLA WITH
CACAO NIBS AND BITTERSWEET CHOCOLATE

I wake up every morning craving coffee . . . and chocolate. I've discovered, however, that nourishing oneself on rich sweets first thing on a daily basis is a recipe for regret. That's when I came up with this breakfast bowl: peanut butter granola with cacao nibs and chocolate. A tiny grating of bittersweet chocolate over the top makes for a delicious bite and is just enough chocolate to satisfy. *makes about 6 cups granola*

¼ cup pure maple syrup

¼ cup creamy peanut butter

½ cup canola oil or olive oil

2 teaspoons water

2 teaspoons pure vanilla extract

5 cups (450 g) old-fashioned
  rolled oats

¼ cup (50 g) packed brown sugar

Pinch salt

1 cup (140 g) whole almonds, toasted
  and chopped

⅓ cup (38 g) cacao nibs

Bittersweet chocolate, for grating

Adjust the oven racks to the upper and lower thirds of the oven. Preheat the oven to 350°F. Line two baking sheets with parchment paper.

In a large bowl or liquid measuring cup, whisk the maple syrup, peanut butter, canola oil, water, and vanilla until smooth. In a large bowl, mix the oats, brown sugar, and salt. Add the wet ingredients to the dry and stir well, making sure the oats are fully coated with the peanut butter mixture.

Spread the oats evenly on the prepared baking sheets, and bake 20 to 30 minutes, stirring often, until the oats are golden brown and no longer wet. Halfway through baking, reposition the baking sheets, moving the top one to the bottom oven rack and the bottom to the top, and rotate the pans 180 degrees.

Transfer the baking sheets to wire racks and let the granola cool, stirring once or twice. Add the almonds and cacao nibs to the cooled granola. Serve with yogurt or milk and grate the chocolate over the top to taste.

MAPLE-CINNAMON GRANOLA

I have spent many hours working in coffeehouses, either as barista or baker. Almost every shop had a little kitchen tucked in the back, where ovens cranked out early A.M. meals: scones, muffins, quiche, and coffee cake. I loved the mornings that granola was included in that lineup. Seven minutes after the trays of oats went in the oven, a faint whiff of cinnamon would weave its way through the store, tempting the line of hungry patrons. Four minutes later the aroma would hit like a flame, leaving no nose untouched. Our minds raced with holiday memories: coming in from the cold and finding a fire ready, with cookies beside it. Together, we would all breathe a collective sigh of nostalgia. *makes about 6 cups granola*

½ cup pure maple syrup

½ cup olive oil or canola oil

1 tablespoon water

1 tablespoon pure vanilla extract

5 cups (450 g) old-fashioned rolled oats

¼ cup (50 g) packed brown sugar

1 teaspoon ground cinnamon

¼ teaspoon salt

Adjust the oven racks to the upper and lower thirds of the oven. Preheat the oven to 350°F. Line two baking sheets with parchment paper.

In a large bowl or liquid measuring cup, mix the maple syrup, olive oil, water, and vanilla. In a large bowl, mix the oats, sugar, cinnamon, and salt. Add the wet ingredients to the dry and stir well, making sure the oats are fully coated.

Spread the oats evenly between the prepared baking sheets and bake 18 to 25 minutes, stirring often, until the oats are golden brown and no longer wet. Halfway through baking, reposition the baking sheets, moving the top one to the bottom oven rack and the bottom of the top, and rotate the pans 180 degrees.

Transfer the baking sheets to wire racks and let the granola cool, stirring once or twice.

NOTES: This recipe is simple and can be easily tweaked to accommodate your breakfast preferences. Here the maple syrup sweetens the oats, but honey can be used instead. The olive oil's peppery note is balanced by the sugars, but can be swapped for canola oil for a more straightforward taste. Cinnamon and vanilla extract can be removed or supplemented: almond extract, cardamom, Chinese five-spice, and ground ginger are all good starting places.

I prefer my granola in smaller pieces, so I stir it often while it is baking to break up the oats. If you like your granola in larger clusters, simply stir the granola once when switching the pans. In either case, make sure you stir the granola in the corners frequently to prevent burning.

When I add nuts to my granola, I toast them separately because I've found they brown much quicker than the oats.

This is a great base recipe to eat as is or personalize with whatever add-ins you like. I stir in 2 cups total of add-ins to one full recipe of granola. One of my favorite ways to eat it is to add 1 cup of toasted pecans and 1 cup of dried cherries, and serve it with yogurt.

ORANGE-CHOCOLATE SCONES

I was in my early twenties and had never eaten a proper scone. My initial encounters had all been tasteless affairs: coffee-chain-store scones that crumbled all over my lap when I bit into them and left me frantically guzzling down coffee as I tried to swallow the dry, sugary pieces. I took to eating muffins and banana bread and wrote off scones entirely.

All that changed one crisp fall day, when I was working the morning shift at the Blue Heron. We were in between rushes, and I was quickly trying to slurp down my iced vanilla latte before the next line of people marched in. Colleen pulled out a baking tray from the oven, and I'll never forget that sight. Beautiful, creamy white triangles glittering with sugar and speckled with dark chocolate and orange zest made their way to the wire racks. The flaky, buttery layers called to me, and I decided I owed them another chance. One blessed bite later I was hooked for life. *makes 8 scones*

2¼ cups (320 g) all-purpose flour

1 tablespoon baking powder

2 tablespoons sugar, plus more for sprinkling

2 teaspoons grated orange zest

½ teaspoon salt

¼ cup Crème Fraîche (page 305) or sour cream

¼ cup orange juice

½ teaspoon pure vanilla extract

1 large egg

12 tablespoons (1½ sticks; 170 g) unsalted butter, cold and cut into ½-inch pieces

4 ounces (113 g) bittersweet chocolate, chopped into small pieces

Heavy cream for brushing

Adjust an oven rack to the lower middle position. Preheat the oven to 400°F. Stack two baking sheets on top of each other and line the top sheet with parchment paper.

In a large bowl, whisk the flour, baking powder, 2 tablespoons sugar, orange zest, and salt. In a medium bowl or liquid measuring cup, whisk the crème fraîche, orange juice, vanilla, and egg.

Add the butter to the dry ingredients and use a pastry cutter to cut it into the mixture until the flour-coated pieces are the size of peas. Add the wet ingredients and fold with a spatula until just combined. Add the bittersweet chocolate, gently folding it into the dough.

CONTINUED

Transfer the dough to a lightly floured surface and knead until it comes together, 4 to 6 times, adding flour as necessary, as the dough will be sticky. Pat the dough gently into a square and roll it into a 12-inch square (again, using flour as necessary). Fold the dough in thirds, similar to a business letter. Fold the dough into thirds again, making a square. Transfer it to a floured sheet pan or plate and put it in the freezer for 10 minutes.

Return the dough to the floured surface, roll it into a 12-inch square, and fold it business letter style. Place the dough seam side down and gently roll it into a 12 by 4-inch rectangle. With a sharp knife, cut it crosswise into 4 equal rectangles, then cut each rectangle diagonally into 2 triangles (see page 47). Transfer the triangles to the prepared baking sheet.

Brush the tops with a little heavy cream, making sure it doesn't drip down the sides and sprinkle the tops generously with sugar. Bake 18 to 25 minutes, rotating the pan halfway through, until the tops and bottoms are light golden brown. Transfer the sheet pan to a wire rack and let the scones cool 10 minutes before serving.

NOTES: Putting another baking sheet nestled directly underneath the one the scones are on helps keep the bottoms of the scones from browning too quickly before they fully bake. If you like the bottoms extra crisp, you can just use one pan.

CRÈME FRAÎCHE SCONES

I had been making scones the same way for years—an adaptation of Ina Garten's Strawberry Scones from her first cookbook, *The Barefoot Contessa*. However, I changed things up after stumbling upon a genius idea from *Cook's Illustrated*. Their scone recipe included folding the dough over several times to create multiple flaky layers. I applied this technique to my tried-and-true recipe, along with replacing the heavy cream with crème fraîche. Crème fraîche is similar to sour cream, but is less sour and has a more nuanced flavor. These scones bake up tender, with just a hint of tang, and the addition of crème fraîche is divine. ***makes 8 scones***

2¼ cups (320 g) all-purpose flour

1 tablespoon baking powder

2 tablespoons sugar, plus more for sprinkling

½ teaspoon salt

½ cup Crème Fraîche (page 305)

½ teaspoon pure vanilla extract

1 large egg

12 tablespoons (1½ sticks; 170 g) unsalted butter, cold, and cut into ½-inch pieces

Heavy cream for brushing

Adjust an oven rack to the lower middle position. Preheat the oven to 400°F. Stack two baking sheets on top of each other and line the top sheet with parchment paper.

In a large bowl, whisk the flour, baking powder, 2 tablespoons sugar, and salt. In a medium bowl or liquid measuring cup, whisk the crème fraîche, vanilla, and egg.

Add the butter to the dry ingredients and use a pastry cutter to cut it into the mixture until the flour-coated pieces are the size of peas. Add the wet ingredients and fold with a spatula until just combined.

Transfer the dough to a lightly floured surface and knead until it comes together, 4 to 6 times, adding flour as necessary if the dough is sticky. Pat the dough gently into a square and roll it into a 12-inch square (again, using flour as necessary). Fold the dough in thirds similar to a business letter. Fold the dough into thirds again, making a square. Transfer to a floured sheet pan or plate and put it in the freezer for 10 minutes.

Return the dough to the floured surface. Roll it into a 12-inch square and fold it business letter style. Place it seam side down and gently roll into a 12 by 4-inch rectangle. With a sharp knife, cut the rectangle crosswise into 4 equal rectangles, then

CONTINUED

cut each rectangle diagonally into 2 triangles (page 47). Transfer the triangles to the prepared baking sheet.

Brush the tops with a little heavy cream, making sure it doesn't drip down the sides and sprinkle the tops generously with sugar. Bake 18 to 25 minutes, rotating the pan halfway through, until the tops and bottoms are light golden brown.

Transfer the sheet pan to a wire rack and let the scones cool 10 minutes before serving.

VARIATION

crème fraîche scones with berries · If your berries are large, chop them into bite-size pieces. After rolling the dough into a square the second time, scatter 1 cup of berries or berry pieces over the top, pressing them down gently into the dough. If the berries are especially tart or out of season, sprinkle 2 tablespoons of sugar over them. Using a bench scraper, loosen the dough from the work surface and roll it into a cylinder, like a jelly-roll log, to help incorporate the berries. Place the cylinder seam side down and press it into a 12 by 4-inch rectangle. Continue with the recipe.

NOTES: Putting another baking sheet nestled directly underneath the one the scones are on helps keep the bottoms of the scones from browning too quickly before they fully bake. If you like the bottoms extra crisp, you can just use one pan.

If you don't have crème fraîche, you can substitute either ¼ cup sour cream mixed with ¼ cup heavy cream or ½ cup heavy cream.

PUMPKIN SCONES

Pumpkin is often associated with cold weather and the holiday season. These scones came about for both those reasons: I find baking in the autumn months a delightful pastime, and scones are a must when family is in town to visit and celebrate. Pumpkin, cinnamon, ginger, and nutmeg all folded up between flaky layers makes the perfect treat for a cool fall morning or a blistery winter afternoon, but if I find you baking them in the middle of July, I won't even blink an eye. *makes 8 scones*

2¼ cups (320 g) all-purpose flour

⅓ cup (66 g) sugar

1 tablespoon baking powder

1 teaspoon ground cinnamon

½ teaspoon ground ginger

¼ teaspoon grated nutmeg

½ teaspoon salt

½ cup unsweetened pumpkin puree

⅓ cup heavy cream, plus more for brushing

1 large egg

1 large egg yolk

½ teaspoon pure vanilla extract

12 tablespoons (1½ sticks; 170 g) unsalted butter, cold and cut into ½-inch pieces

MAPLE FROSTING

⅓ cup pure maple syrup

1 cup (113 g) confectioners' sugar

½ teaspoon pure vanilla extract

Pinch salt

Adjust an oven rack to the lower middle position. Preheat the oven to 400°F. Stack two baking sheets on top of each other and line the top sheet with parchment paper.

In a large bowl, whisk the flour, sugar, baking powder, cinnamon, ginger, nutmeg, and salt. In a medium bowl or liquid measuring cup, whisk the pumpkin puree, heavy cream, egg, egg yolk, and vanilla.

Add the butter to the dry ingredients and use a pastry cutter to cut it into the mixture until the flour-coated pieces are the size of peas. Add the wet ingredients and fold with a spatula until just combined.

Transfer the dough to a lightly floured surface, and knead until it comes together, 4 to 6 times, adding flour as necessary if the dough is sticky. Pat the dough gently into a small square and roll it into a 12-inch square (again, using flour as necessary). Fold the dough in thirds similar to a business letter. Fold the dough into thirds again, making a square. Transfer it to a floured sheet pan or plate and put it in the freezer for 10 minutes.

CONTINUED

Return the dough to the floured surface. Roll it into a 12-inch square and fold it business letter style. Place the dough seam side down and gently roll into a 12 by 4-inch rectangle. With a sharp knife (or bench scraper), cut the rectangle crosswise into 4 equal rectangles, then cut each rectangle diagonally into 2 triangles (see facing page). Transfer the triangles to the prepared baking sheet.

Brush the tops with a little heavy cream, making sure it doesn't drip down the sides. Bake 18 to 25 minutes, rotating the pan halfway through, until the tops and bottoms are golden brown.

Transfer the sheet pan to a wire rack and let the scones cool slightly. Top with the Maple Frosting.

FOR THE MAPLE FROSTING: In a small bowl, whisk the maple syrup, confectioners' sugar, vanilla, and salt until smooth.

NOTES: Putting another baking sheet nestled directly underneath the one the scones are on helps keep the bottoms of the scones from browning too quickly before they fully bake. If you like the bottoms extra crisp, you can just use one pan.

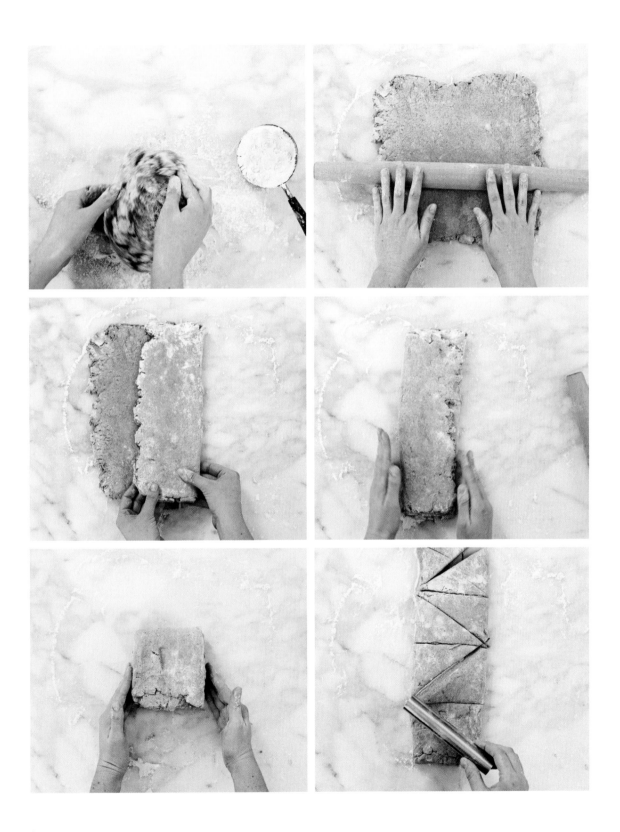

DUTCH BABY

When I was growing up, big breakfasts were a weekend affair. During the week it was every child for herself; my morning meal usually consisted of a heaping bowl of cereal overflowing with milk. Saturdays, though, could get fancy. My mom would whip up some pancakes, and we would slather those warm golden circles with maple syrup, all the cares of the week disappearing into that river of golden sugar and a side of bacon.

Years later, and Saturdays still hold their sophisticated edge. Dutch Babies are one of our favorite ways to kick off the weekend, and we rejoice when the piping-hot skillet is pulled from the oven, displaying an elevated pancake of glory. *makes 3 to 4 servings*

1 cup (142 g) all-purpose flour	1 cup whole milk
2 tablespoons cornstarch	1 teaspoon pure vanilla extract
1 tablespoon sugar	4 tablespoons (57 g) unsalted butter, cold
½ teaspoon salt	
4 large eggs	Confectioners' sugar, for dusting

Adjust an oven rack to the middle position. Preheat the oven to 450°F. In a large bowl, whisk the flour, cornstarch, sugar, and salt. In a medium bowl or liquid measuring cup, whisk the eggs, milk, and vanilla until incorporated. Whisk one-third of the wet ingredients into the flour mixture until no lumps remain, then slowly add the remaining wet ingredients, whisking until smooth.

Place the butter into a 10-inch cast-iron skillet and put it in the oven to preheat for 3 to 4 minutes, until the butter melts and starts to sizzle in the pan.

Using an oven mitt, carefully remove the skillet from the oven and pour the batter in. Immediately return the skillet to the oven. Bake 16 to 20 minutes, until the edges are golden brown and crisp and the pancake has risen and puffed (if you like the edges extra crispy, you can bake it a few minutes longer).

Transfer the skillet to a wire rack and sprinkle the pancake with confectioners' sugar. Cut into wedges and serve with Coffee Syrup (page 315).

NOTE: You can add fresh fruit to the Dutch Baby before the batter is poured into the skillet. Put 1 cup berries or a peeled, sliced pear into the hot buttered skillet and sauté for 1 minute. Pour in the batter and bake as directed. Or serve with fresh berries on the side along with some Whipped Cream (page 306) or Crème Fraîche (page 305).

APPLE-BLACKBERRY TURNOVERS

A twist on the classic apple turnover, these buttery, golden triangles also include blackberries and brandy. The blackberries add a slightly tart note that is offset nicely by the sweet apples and flaky pastry. Homemade puff pastry will bring these to the next level, but you can use store-bought in a pinch. *makes 8 turnovers*

1 recipe Rough Puff Pastry (page 75), cut into 2 pieces, or 1 pound store-bought puff pastry

1 cup (150 g) grated Gala apple, about 2 small apples

1 cup (170 g) blackberries, fresh or frozen

⅓ cup (66 g) sugar, plus more for sprinkling

1 teaspoon pure vanilla extract

1 tablespoon brandy

⅛ teaspoon ground cinnamon

Pinch salt

Line a sheet pan with parchment paper.

Put the grated apple, blackberries, sugar, vanilla, brandy, cinnamon, and salt in a medium bowl and stir to combine.

Lightly flour a work surface and roll each piece of the pastry dough into a 10-inch square. Cut each square into four 5-inch squares, for a total of 8 squares. Divide the fruit mixture evenly between the squares of dough. Brush the edges of each square with water, fold the dough to make a triangle, and crimp the edges with a fork to seal. Transfer the triangles to the prepared baking sheet and place the sheet in the freezer while the oven preheats.

Adjust an oven rack to the lower middle position. Preheat the oven to 400°F.

When the oven has preheated, take the baking sheet out of the freezer and brush the tops of the dough lightly but evenly with water, then generously sprinkle with sugar. Bake 20 to 25 minutes, rotating the pan halfway through, until golden brown.

Transfer the turnovers to a wire rack and let cool slightly. Serve warm.

NOTES: I prefer Gala apples, but you can use your favorite apple variety here.

Diced pear is a great substitution for the apples, and frozen blackberries or raspberries will work in the winter months. If using frozen berries, you can add them to the apple mixture still cold.

Freezing the turnovers before baking helps the blackberries from leaking too much, although they will still trickle a bit.

CINNAMON ROLLS

I'm not sure what exactly it is about cinnamon rolls that is so enticing. There is something equally comforting and delicious in those gooey swirled centers that makes it impossible to eat just one. After years of using brioche dough and a basic vanilla glaze, I've finally perfected cinnamon rolls to my liking. My sweet dough recipe, enriched with honey and eggs, makes for a tender base; a hefty amount of cinnamon gives a nice kick and cream cheese keeps the confectioners' sugar in the icing from being cloying. It's one dreamy bun. *makes 12 cinnamon rolls*

1 recipe Sweet Dough (page 77)

½ cup (99 g) packed brown sugar

1 tablespoon ground cinnamon

Pinch salt

2 tablespoons (29 g) unsalted butter, melted and cooled

ICING

8 tablespoons (1 stick; 113 g) unsalted butter, room temperature

4 ounces (114 g) cream cheese, room temperature

1 teaspoon pure vanilla extract

¼ teaspoon salt

1 cup (113 g) confectioners' sugar

Flour a work surface and knead the Sweet Dough 10 to 12 times. Shape the dough into a ball, cover the top lightly with flour, and if your dough has been refrigerated, cover with a tea towel and let it come to room temperature.

Grease a 9 by 13-inch pan; if desired, line with parchment paper (this makes for an easier cleanup).

In a small bowl, mix the brown sugar, cinnamon, and salt.

Roll the dough into a 16 by 12-inch rectangle. Brush the dough with the melted butter and sprinkle the cinnamon-sugar mixture evenly over top, pressing it lightly into the butter so it adheres. Starting at a long side, roll the dough into a tight cylinder. Pinch the seam gently to seal it and position the dough seam side down. Use scissors or a sharp knife to cut the dough into 12 equal pieces (see page 54). Transfer the pieces to the prepared pan and place them cut side up. Cover the pan loosely with plastic wrap and let the dough rise until doubled, 1 to 1½ hours.

Adjust the oven rack to the lower middle position. Preheat the oven to 350°F.

CONTINUED

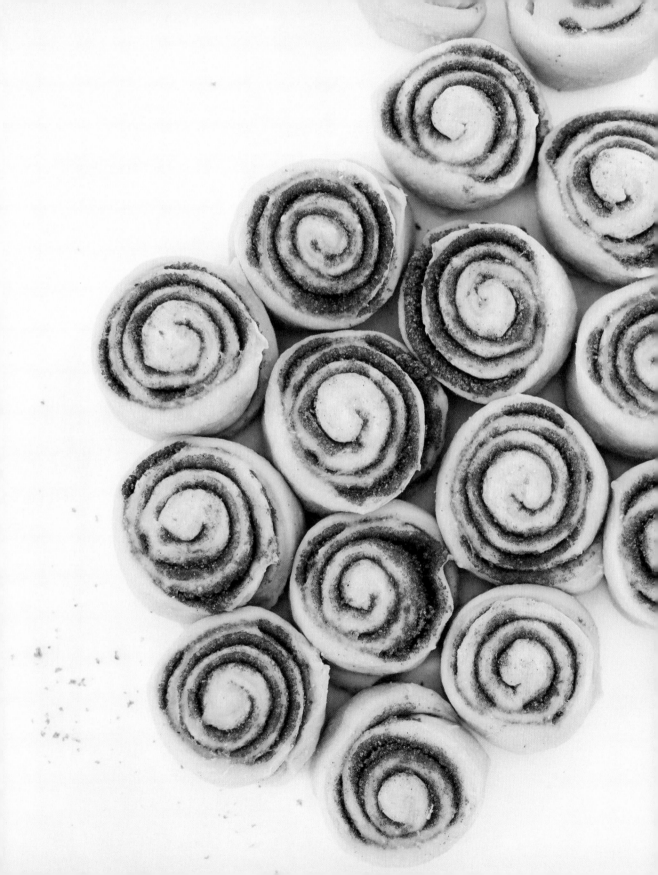

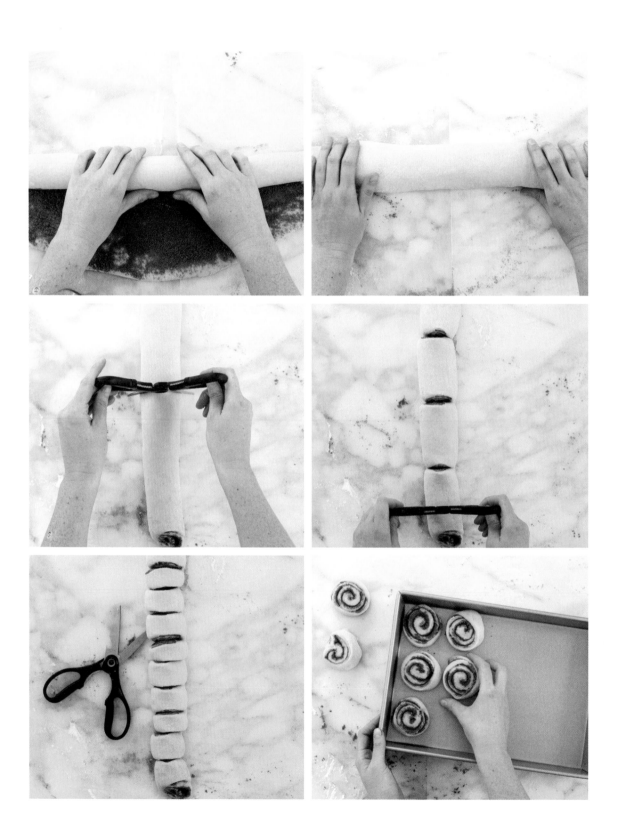

Remove the plastic and bake 27 to 32 minutes, rotating the pan halfway through, until the rolls are golden brown. While the rolls are baking, prepare the icing.

Transfer the pan to a wire rack and let cool for 5 minutes. Using an offset spatula or table knife, apply a thin layer of the cream cheese icing, using about one-third of the mixture. Let the rolls cool for another 15 to 20 minutes. Top with the rest of the icing and serve.

FOR THE ICING: In the bowl of a stand mixer fitted with a paddle, beat the butter and cream cheese on medium until smooth and creamy. Add the vanilla and salt and mix on low to combine. Add the confectioners' sugar and mix on low until combined. Scrape down the sides of the bowl and mix on medium until the icing is light and fluffy, 3 to 4 minutes.

VARIATION

cinnamon roll wreath · Follow the directions for filling and rolling the dough into a log. Carefully move the log to a baking sheet lined with parchment paper. Shape the log into a ring. Using scissors or a sharp knife, make 10 to 11 cuts spaced evenly around the outside of the dough, not cutting all the way through the log. Twist each piece cut side up. Cover loosely with plastic wrap and let rise 1 to 1½ hours, until doubled in size. Brush the top with egg wash then bake in a 350°F oven for 25 to 32 minutes, until golden brown. Top with Confectioners' Sugar Glaze (page 311) and chopped pistachios, if desired.

NOTES: The dough can be cut in 8, 10, or 12 pieces, depending on your preferred size. Add a few minutes to the baking time for larger-size buns.

I like my cinnamon rolls super soft and gooey, so I put a thin layer of the icing over them while they are still very warm. The icing melts into the warm rolls, eliminating any hard corners or edges. If you prefer a little crispy crunch to your cinnamon rolls, you can wait until they have cooled and then top with all the icing. And if you just need to eat them warm, go ahead and smother them with all the icing right from the oven.

CARAMEL ROLLS

Over the years I've made quite a few batches of caramel rolls, only to be disappointed with gummy centers and soggy pecans. Flipping the pan was a safety hazard—hot sticky caramel leaked all over everyone and everything except the rolls themselves. Baking the rolls without the caramel, I discovered, solved a lot of problems. The dough baked up tender, and I could control where the sauce would end up. I toasted the pecans separately, giving each bite a good crunch. A little extra work, but worth all the effort. *makes 12 caramel rolls*

1 recipe Sweet Dough (page 77)

¾ cup (149 g) packed brown sugar

1 teaspoon ground cinnamon

½ teaspoon grated nutmeg

⅛ teaspoon ground cloves

Pinch salt

2 tablespoons (29 g) unsalted butter, melted and cooled slightly

½ cup (57 g) pecan halves, toasted

Caramel Sauce (page 316)

Flour a work surface and knead the Sweet Dough 10 to 12 times. Shape the dough into a ball, cover the top lightly with flour, and if your dough has been refrigerated, cover with a tea towel and let it come to room temperature.

Grease a 9 by 13-inch pan; if desired, line with parchment paper (this makes for an easier cleanup).

In a small bowl, combine the brown sugar, cinnamon, nutmeg, cloves, and salt.

Roll the dough into a 16 by 12-inch rectangle. Brush the dough with the melted butter and sprinkle the brown sugar mixture evenly over the top, pressing it lightly into the butter so it adheres. Starting at a long side, roll the dough into a tight cylinder. Stretch the dough if needed so it is an even width across the whole length. Pinch the seam gently to seal it and position the dough seam side down. Use a scissors or sharp knife to cut the dough into 12 equal pieces (see page 54). Transfer the pieces to the prepared pan and place them cut side up. Cover the pan loosely with plastic wrap and let the dough rise until doubled, 1 to 1½ hours.

Adjust the oven rack to the lower middle position. Preheat the oven to 350°F.

Remove the plastic and bake 30 to 35 minutes, rotating the pan halfway through, until the rolls are golden brown. While the rolls are baking, prepare the caramel sauce.

Transfer the pan to a wire rack and immediately pour half the warm sauce over the rolls and let them sit for 10 to 15 minutes. Stir the pecans into the remaining caramel sauce and pour over the top, covering the rolls evenly. Serve immediately.

CARDAMOM BRAIDED KNOTS

I was introduced to cardamom in college, and the intensity of the spice seemed so exotic to me at the time. My initial taste was in scone form; the bake case at the Blue Heron displayed a cardamom-chocolate version at least once a week, and they ended up being a regular breakfast for me. Even today, cardamom is one of my favorite spices, and I bake with it frequently. It works beautifully in cakes, scones, quick bread, muffins—everything really. I love how the gray-purple flecks look in these braided knots. *makes 8 braided knots*

1 recipe Sweet Dough (page 77)

1½ cups (297 g) sugar

1½ tablespoons ground cardamom

Pinch salt

5 tablespoons (72 g) unsalted butter, melted and cooled

Egg wash (page 14)

Flour a work surface and knead the Sweet Dough 10 to 12 times. Shape the dough into a ball, lightly cover the top with flour, and if your dough is cold, cover with a tea towel and let it come to room temperature.

Line a baking sheet with parchment paper.

In a small bowl, combine the sugar, cardamom, and salt.

Cut the dough into 8 equal pieces. Roll each piece into a ball and loosely cover the balls with plastic wrap. Generously flour your work surface and, working one piece at a time, roll a ball of dough into a 6 by 14-inch rectangle (if you have trouble getting your dough to exactly 14 inches, don't worry; you just want a long rectangle that isn't too thin). Brush the dough with melted butter and sprinkle generously with the sugar mixture, using about 2 heaping tablespoons per piece. Starting at a long side, roll the dough into a tight cylinder and place it on the prepared baking sheet. When all eight pieces of dough have been formed into logs, place the baking sheet in the fridge for 10 to 15 minutes (this will help make cutting the dough easier).

Trim about ¼ inch off both ends of each chilled log and discard. Working with one log at a time, use scissors or a sharp knife to gently cut the log in half lengthwise, so the layers of dough and filling are visible. With the cut sides facing up, gently press together one end of each half, and then lift the right half over the left half, letting the layers fan out as you twist them. Continue until you have twisted the entire roll.

CONTINUED

Press the ends together, forming a point. Shape the twisted dough into a small circle, overlapping the ends to make a sort of cross shape. Bring the bottom end up and over the top through the center of the knot. Tuck the top end underneath the bottom of the knot and pinch the two ends together (see facing page). Place the knots back on the prepared baking sheet, cover lightly with plastic wrap, and let rise slightly, 1 to 1½ hours.

Adjust the oven rack to the middle position. Preheat the oven to 350°F.

Brush the knots carefully with egg wash, trying not to disturb the sugar filling, and bake 20 to 25 minutes, until the knots are golden brown. As the knots rise and bake, they will leak a little sugar and butter, just like cinnamon rolls do. Best eaten the day they are made.

NOTE: I find a scissors much easier to use than a knife when cutting the dough; it makes much cleaner cuts.

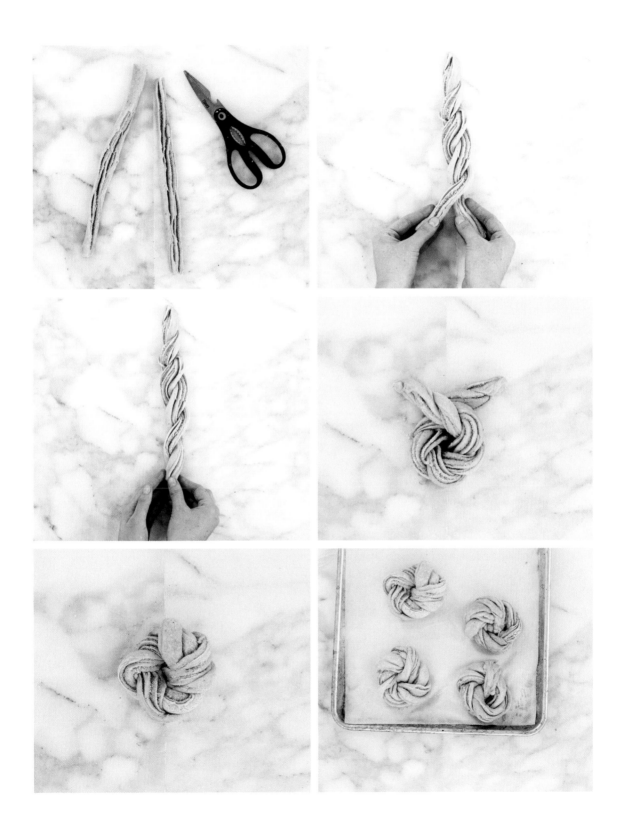

BRAIDED CHOCOLATE SWIRL BREAD

I've fallen in love with braided bread: There is something about the lines of color in the dough, all twisted and wrapped around each other, that is absolutely beautiful to me. This particular loaf uses sweet dough, which can be made ahead of time, dividing kitchen duty into manageable segments. The bread bakes up tall, and I like to eat it plain the day it's made or toasted and soaked in butter later in the week. I'm also betting it would make an excellent French toast. *serves 6 to 8*

1 recipe Sweet Dough (page 77)

4 ounces (113 g) bittersweet chocolate

6 tablespoons (86 g) unsalted butter

½ cup (99 g) packed brown sugar

2 tablespoons Dutch process cocoa powder

¼ teaspoon salt

Flour a work surface and knead the Sweet Dough 10 to 12 times. Shape the dough into a ball, cover the top lightly with flour, and if the dough is cold, cover with a tea towel and let it come to room temperature.

Line a 9-inch loaf pan or a Pullman pan with a parchment sling (page 15).

In a small saucepan, heat the bittersweet chocolate and butter over low heat until melted and smooth. Whisk in the brown sugar, cocoa powder, and salt until a smooth paste forms. Set aside to cool. Roll the dough into a 18 by 14-inch rectangle. Use an offset spatula to spread the chocolate mixture over the rectangle, leaving an inch border on all the sides. Starting with a long side, roll the dough into a tight cylinder. Pinch the seam gently to seal it. Trim about ¾ inch off each end of the roll and discard. Using scissors or a sharp knife, gently cut the roll in half lengthwise, so the layers of dough and filling are visible. With the cut sides facing up, gently press together one end of each half, and then lift the right half over the left half, and continue until you have twisted the entire roll (see page 61). Press the ends together. Carefully transfer the dough into the prepared pan. It will seem too big for the pan, but twist and turn it to fit (see page 62). Cover with plastic wrap and let rise in a warm place for 1 to 1 ½ hours, until the dough has risen about an inch over the lip of the pan (if using a Pullman pan, the dough will have risen just below the top of the pan).

Adjust the oven rack to the lower middle position. Preheat the oven to 350°F.

Remove the plastic and bake 40 to 55 minutes, or until a wooden skewer or toothpick inserted in the middle comes out clean or the bread registers 200°F on an instant read thermometer.

CONTINUED

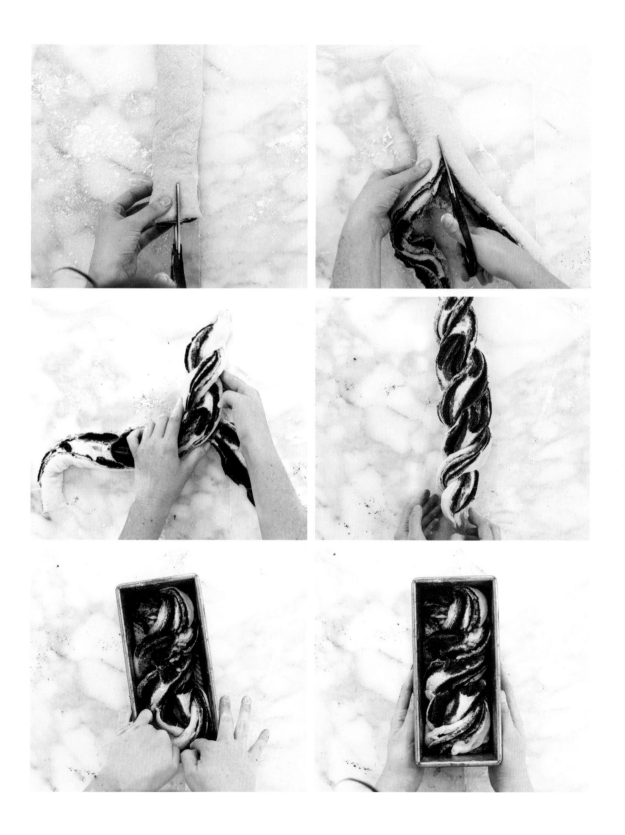

Transfer the pan to a wire rack and let cool for 10 minutes. Carefully remove the bread from the pan and onto the rack to finish cooling. Wait until the bread has cooled completely before slicing.

NOTE: If the top of the bread is turning dark too quickly, cover loosely with a piece of foil.

Because the bread uses so much dough, an 8-inch pan will be too small.

CREAM CHEESE DANISH

Before there was a coffeehouse chain on every corner, the only establishment in the suburbs to take your children to and let them be loud was McDonald's. A few neighborhood moms, mine included, would take us one morning a week. There the adults would sit, sipping hot coffee while all the kids were placed at a nearby booth, coloring and begging for more greasy hash browns. I remember my mom often ordering a cheese Danish with her coffee, the sight of it making me wrinkle my nose in horror. Cream cheese was an ingredient in onion dip or something far worse. Why would it taste any better covered in sugar? Sadly, I was almost thirty before I finally understood. *makes 6 danish pastries*

½ recipe Easy Danish Dough (page 71)

6 ounces (170 g) cream cheese, room temperature

¼ cup (50 g) sugar

1 large egg

½ teaspoon pure vanilla extract

2 teaspoons grated lemon zest (optional)

Pinch salt

1 tablespoon (15 g) unsalted butter, melted and cooled

Egg wash (page 14)

Confectioners' Sugar Glaze (page 311)

In the bowl of a stand mixer fitted with a paddle, beat the cream cheese on medium speed until smooth. Scrape down the sides of the bowl and add the sugar, egg, vanilla, lemon zest (if using), salt, and butter and mix on low until completely combined. Cover the bowl and put in the fridge until ready to use.

Line a baking sheet with parchment paper.

Flour a work surface and roll the Easy Danish Dough into a 10 by14-inch rectangle, flouring as needed so the dough doesn't stick. Use a pastry cutter to trim any rough edges of the rectangle and discard them. Cut the dough in half horizontally and cut each half into thirds, for a total of six pieces. Place a heaping tablespoon of the cream cheese filling in the center of each piece. Fold up the opposite corners of the dough and pinch together to seal, so all four corners are pinched in the middle of the pastry.

Place the shaped dough on the prepared baking sheet and brush each piece with the egg wash. Loosely cover the dough with plastic, and let the dough rise until puffy (feeling similar to a marshmallow when pressed), about 1½ hours.

CONTINUED

Adjust an oven rack to the middle position. Preheat the oven to 350°F.

If the corners of the dough have separated while rising, gently pinch them back together. Bake 15 to 17 minutes, until the Danish pastries are golden brown.

Transfer the baking sheet to a wire rack and let cool. Drizzle the Danish pastries with Confectioners' Sugar Glaze.

NOTES: You can add fresh or frozen berries, a swirl of jam or chocolate ganache, and even a handful of raisins to the Danish along with the cream cheese filling. Just remember not to overfill or it will ooze out of the pastry as it bakes.

Recipe can easily be doubled to make 12 Danish pastries.

APRICOT DANISH

These spiraled pastries are just a bit fancier than their cream cheese counterparts, and not that much harder to put together. They are a beautiful addition to any breakfast or brunch table, and I love making them around the holidays for friends and neighbors. Any flavored jam can be substituted for the apricot. *makes 8 danish pastries*

½ recipe Easy Danish Dough (71)

Egg wash (page 14)

¼ cup apricot jam (or any other flavor you like)

Confectioners' Sugar Glaze (page 311)

Flour a work surface and roll the Easy Danish Dough into a 10 by 14-inch rectangle, flouring as needed so the dough doesn't stick. Use a pastry cutter to trim any rough edges of the rectangle and discard them. Cut the dough vertically into 8 even pieces.

Line a baking sheet with parchment paper.

Hold one end of a dough strip in place with one hand. Using your other hand, twist the strip into a spiral. Curl the spiral strip into a snail shape. Tuck the loose end of the strip underneath the snail (see page 69). Place the shaped dough on the prepared baking sheet, spacing the snails 2 inches apart. Cover lightly with plastic wrap and let rise until puffy (similar to a marshmallow when pressed), about 1½ hours.

Adjust an oven rack to the lower middle position. Preheat the oven to 350°F.

Just before baking, gently press the center of each dough snail to make a spot for the jam, trying not to push on the rest of the dough. Lightly brush the dough with egg wash and then place a scant teaspoon of jam in the center of each piece. Bake 18 to 20 minutes, until the Danish pastries are golden brown.

Transfer the baking sheet to a wire rack and let cool slightly. Drizzle the Danish pastries with Confectioners' Sugar Glaze.

NOTE: This recipe can easily be doubled to make 16 Danish pastries.

EASY DANISH DOUGH

This recipe is more hasty than the original version it stems from, but still is a good pass for the real thing. The butter and egg yolks contribute rich flavor, the turns many flaky layers. Because this is a yeasted dough, it is also has a wonderful light texture. Traditional Danish dough is often flavored with cardamom, and I recommend adding it if you are a fan of the spice. *makes about 2 pounds (908 g) of dough*

¾ cup whole milk, warm (100–110°F)

1 large egg, room temperature

2 large egg yolks, room temperature

1 teaspoon pure vanilla extract

2½ cups (355 g) all-purpose flour

2¼ teaspoons instant yeast

2 tablespoons sugar

1 teaspoon salt

1 teaspoon ground cardamom (optional)

4 tablespoons (½ stick; 57 g) unsalted butter, room temperature

12 tablespoons (1½ sticks; 170 g) unsalted butter, cold and cut into about 20 pieces

Grease a large bowl.

In a large liquid measuring cup, combine the milk, egg, yolk, and vanilla.

In the bowl of a stand mixer fitted with a paddle, mix the flour, yeast, sugar, salt, and cardamom (if using) on low. Add the room temperature butter and mix on low until it is incorporated into the flour and no pieces are visible. Add the cold butter and mix on low, until it is broken down and smashed a bit, but still in ½-inch pieces. Add the milk mixture and mix on low until combined. The dough will be very sticky and there will be visible lumps of butter. Using a spatula, scrape the dough into the prepared bowl and cover tightly with plastic wrap and refrigerate overnight, or up to 3 days.

The next morning, transfer the dough to a well-floured work surface. Knead 10 to 12 times, until the dough forms a ball. Cover the top lightly with flour and cover with a tea towel, let rest until it comes to room temperature. Pat the dough into a 6-inch square and roll into a 16 by 20-inch rectangle. If the dough sticks at all, sprinkle more flour underneath it. Brush any excess flour off the dough, and, using a bench scraper, fold the short ends of the dough over the middle to make three layers, similar to a business letter. This is the first turn.

CONTINUED

Flip the dough over (seam side down) and roll into an 8 by 16-inch rectangle. Fold the short ends over the middle, business letter style. Repeat the steps again, for a total of four turns.

On the last turn, gently use the rolling pin to compress the layers together slightly. Wrap the dough tightly in plastic wrap and chill for at least 1 hour before using or keep refrigerated for 2 days.

NOTES: It is important for the Danish dough to come to room temperature before you roll it out, or the butter will not incorporate correctly.

This dough can be frozen, but it doesn't rise quite as nicely as when it's fresh.

If the dough is not used right away after being rolled and turned, it will puff up in the refrigerator. This will make it a little harder to roll out, but you will still have good results.

ROUGH PUFF PASTRY

Puff pastry can be rather intimidating. It's a dough that depends on patience and time, and making it requires commitment and precision. There is, however, a shortcut to puff pastry. This quick adaptation is not as obsessive or exacting as the real thing, but still contains rich, flaky layers, just like the more labor-intensive version. Rolling and turning the dough can take some practice, but once you taste those buttery layers, the store-bought version will no longer be an option. *makes about 2 pounds (908 g) of puff pastry*

¾ pound (3 sticks; 339 g) unsalted butter, cold and cut into 16 to 20 pieces

½ teaspoon lemon juice

2 cups (284 g) all-purpose flour

½ teaspoon salt

1 tablespoon sugar

Put the butter in a small bowl and place it in the freezer. Fill a medium liquid measuring cup with water and add plenty of ice. Let the butter and water cool for 5 to 10 minutes.

In a small liquid measuring cup, combine the lemon juice and ¼ cup of the ice water.

In the bowl of a stand mixer fitted with a paddle, mix the flour, salt, and sugar on low. Add the butter and mix on low until slightly incorporated. The butter will be a bit smashed and all different sizes, most about half their original size.

Add the lemon juice mixture and mix on low until the dough just holds together and looks shaggy. If the dough is still really dry and not coming together, add ice water, 1 tablespoon at a time, until it just starts to hold.

Transfer the dough to a lightly floured work surface and flatten it slightly into a square. Gather any loose/dry pieces and place them on top. Gently fold the dough over onto itself and flatten again. Repeat this process 5 or 6 more times, until all the loose pieces are worked into the dough. Be very gentle with your movements, being careful not to overwork the dough. Flatten the dough one last time into a 6-inch square. Transfer the dough to a floured sheet pan or plate and sprinkle the top of the dough with flour. Place the dough in the fridge and chill until firm, 20 minutes.

Return the dough to the lightly floured work surface and roll it into an 8 by 16-inch

CONTINUED

rectangle. If the dough sticks at all, sprinkle more flour underneath it. Brush any excess flour off the dough, and, using a bench scraper, fold the short ends of the dough over the middle to make three layers similar to a business letter. This is the first turn.

Your dough may still look quite shaggy, but don't worry, it will become smooth and even out as you go. If your rectangle is a little off (7 by 15 inches, for example), don't stress about it. Each turn will get easier.

Flip the dough over (seam side down), give the dough a quarter turn and roll away from you, this time into a 6 by 16-inch rectangle. Fold the short ends over the middle, business letter style. This is the second turn.

Sprinkle the top of the dough with flour and return it to the sheet pan and refrigerate for 20 minutes.

Return the dough to the work surface and repeat the process of folding the dough, creating the third and fourth turns. On the last turn, gently use a rolling pin to compress the layers together slightly. Wrap tightly in plastic wrap and chill for at least 1 hour before using; keep refrigerated for up to 2 days.

NOTE: The dough can be frozen for up to 2 months in a freezer-safe bag. When ready to use, transfer the dough to the refrigerator and let thaw overnight (8 to 12 hours).

SWEET DOUGH

The first yeasted dough I ever made that was enriched with both eggs and honey came from Jeff Hertzberg and Zoë François's wonderful book, *The New Artisan Bread in Five Minutes a Day*. Their version is a no-knead dough that keeps for days in the refrigerator. When I developed this recipe, I knew I wanted something along similar lines—a dough that didn't require a lot of work and could be made a few days in advance if need be. This dough is made right in the stand mixer and doesn't require a dough hook. The ingredients mix together easily, and then the dough is gently folded over itself a few times during the rise time, which helps form a fine, even crumb. *makes about 2½ pounds (1,135 g) of dough*

4 large eggs, room temperature

¾ cup whole milk, warm (100–110°F)

¼ cup honey

4 cups (568 g) all-purpose flour

2¼ teaspoons instant yeast

2 teaspoons salt

10 tablespoons (1¼ sticks; 142 g) unsalted butter, room temperature, cut into 1-inch pieces

Grease a large bowl.

In a large liquid measuring cup, combine the eggs, milk, and honey.

In the bowl of a stand mixer fitted with a paddle, mix the flour, yeast, and salt and stir on low to combine. Add the egg mixture and mix on low to combine. With the mixer on low, add the butter, one piece at a time. When all the butter has been added, increase the speed to medium and beat the butter into the dough, until all the little butter pieces are incorporated, 1 minute. Transfer the dough to the prepared bowl. The dough will be very sticky and you will need a spatula to scrape the dough into the bowl.

Cover the bowl with plastic wrap and let rise for 30 minutes. Place your fingers or a spatula underneath the dough and gently pull the dough up and fold it back over itself. Turn the bowl and repeat this folding again (see page 78). Continue 6 to 8 more times, until all the dough has been folded over on itself. Re-cover the bowl with plastic and let rise for 30 minutes. Repeat this series of folding 3 more times, for a rise time of 2 hours and a total of 4 foldings. Tightly cover the bowl with plastic wrap and refrigerate overnight or up to 72 hours.

NOTE: The dough can be used right away (after the initial 2-hour rise) if needed. I find it is much easier to work with after it has been refrigerated overnight.

chapter two

QUICK BREADS, MUFFINS + EVERYDAY CAKES

I list quick breads, muffins, and simple cakes in the "all-day eating" category. The treats in this group of sweets make a delicious start to the morning, but they taste just as good in the late afternoon with a last cup of coffee or even in the twilight hours, pondering life with lingering guests. They are simpler to put together than a morning pastry or a party cake, and while they may not often be reserved for special breakfast get-togethers or fancy dinners, they still have their place in any kitchen. Reliable and consistent, these treats are faithful companions to our everyday life.

WHOLE WHEAT BANANA-CHOCOLATE MUFFINS

Baked goods made with only whole wheat flour can sometimes be dense and dry, but this delicious muffin recipe is an exception. Maple syrup and mashed bananas help keep the batter moist, and chopped chocolate gives each bite a good reason to take another. I make these frequently throughout the year, but especially after the holidays when I'm still addicted to sugar and need something to help ease the transition to more virtuous soups and salads. *makes 20 to 21 muffins*

2½ cups (390 g) whole wheat flour

1 teaspoon baking soda

1 teaspoon baking powder

½ teaspoon salt

¾ cup canola or olive oil

1 cup buttermilk

1 cup mashed banana
(about 3 bananas)

1 large egg

2 teaspoons pure vanilla extract

½ cup maple syrup

¼ cup (50 g) sugar

1 cup (150 g) diced banana
(about 1½ bananas)

1 cup (170 g) chocolate chips

Turbinado sugar, for sprinkling

Adjust an oven rack to the lower middle position. Preheat the oven to 375°F. Place liners in two standard 12-cup muffins tins, filling 21 of the cups.

Whisk the flour, baking soda, baking powder, and salt in a large bowl. Make a well in the center.

In a large bowl or liquid measuring cup, whisk the oil, buttermilk, mashed banana, egg, vanilla, maple syrup, and sugar until completely combined. Pour the wet ingredients into the well in the dry ingredients and mix gently until almost combined. Fold in the diced banana and the chocolate until just incorporated, being careful not to overwork the batter (the batter should not be completely smooth; there should still be some visible lumps and bumps). The batter will be very runny.

Scoop the batter into the prepared tins, filling the cups about two-thirds full. Sprinkle with turbinado sugar. Bake 14 to 18 minutes, until the edges are golden brown and a wooden skewer or toothpick inserted in the center comes out clean.

NOTES: If you like a little crunch to your muffins, add ½ cup (57 g) of toasted chopped pecans to the batter along with the chocolate.

This recipe makes quite a few muffins, but they freeze well.

BLUEBERRY MUFFINS

Blueberry muffins were a staple in our house. I remember a tower of prepackaged muffin mix stacked next to the cereal in our cupboard above the stove. Whenever my mom would take one down, we would beg her to let us help stir everything together. She taught us how to measure oil and crack eggs and not to overmix. The tiny specks of blueberries poking out in the batter dazzled us, and we devoured the muffins straight out of the oven, still warm and soaked in butter.

I started making muffins from scratch when I worked at the Blue Heron Coffeehouse, and the recipe has been used everywhere I have worked. Over the years I've made changes: adding a little more sugar and fruit and a bit of butter along with the oil. It's much better than breakfast out of a box, and you'll still get that same nostalgic feeling. *makes 15 to 16 muffins*

2½ cups (355 g) all-purpose flour

1 teaspoon baking soda

1 teaspoon baking powder

½ teaspoon salt

2 teaspoons grated lemon zest

4 tablespoons (½ stick; 57 g) unsalted butter, melted and slightly cooled

½ cup canola oil

1¼ cups buttermilk

2 teaspoons pure vanilla extract

¾ cup (149 g) sugar, plus extra for sprinkling

1 large egg

¼ cup lemon juice

2 heaping cups (283 g) blueberries, fresh or frozen

Adjust an oven rack to the lower middle position. Preheat the oven to 375°F. Place liners in two standard 12-cup muffins tins, filling 16 of the cups.

Whisk the flour, baking soda, baking powder, salt, and lemon zest in a large bowl. Make a well in the center.

In a large bowl or liquid measuring cup, whisk the butter, oil, buttermilk, vanilla, sugar, egg, and lemon juice until completely combined. Pour the wet ingredients into the well in the dry ingredients and mix gently until almost combined. Fold in the blueberries until just incorporated, being careful not to overwork the batter (the batter should not be completely smooth; there should still be some visible lumps and bumps).

Scoop the batter into the prepared tins, filling the muffin cups two-thirds full. Sprinkle the tops generously with sugar. Bake 18 to 22 minutes, until the edges are golden brown and a wooden skewer or toothpick inserted in the center comes out clean.

BERRY MUFFINS WITH STREUSEL

Every morning at Bordertown Coffee I would make a huge tray of blueberry muffins, along with another batch that highlighted a different fruit flavor each day. Blackberries, peaches, rhubarb, and cherries all had a chance to sing, along with chocolate and nuts. I mixed and matched them in various combinations, and our customers loved the variety. At home I normally stick with raspberries or blackberries in this recipe, but you can create any streusel muffin of your dreams. Plain fruit works here, or try a combination of chocolate and nuts. Cinnamon can be swapped for cardamom, ginger, or nutmeg. The tops can be covered with streusel, or just a sprinkling of sugar. There is plenty of room for experimentation. *makes 15 to 16 muffins*

2½ cups (355 g) all-purpose flour

1 teaspoon baking soda

1 teaspoon baking powder

½ teaspoon salt

¾ teaspoon ground cinnamon

4 tablespoons (½ stick; 57 g) unsalted butter, melted and slightly cooled

½ cup canola oil

1¼ cups buttermilk

2 teaspoons pure vanilla extract

¾ cup (149 g) sugar, plus more for sprinkling

1 large egg

2 heaping cups (283 g) raspberries or chopped blackberries, fresh or frozen

Streusel (page 312)

Adjust an oven rack to the lower middle position. Preheat the oven to 375°F. Place liners in two standard 12-cup muffins tins, filling 16 of the cups.

Whisk the flour, baking soda, baking powder, salt, and cinnamon in a large bowl. Make a well in the center.

In a large bowl or liquid measuring cup, whisk the butter, canola oil, buttermilk, vanilla, sugar, and egg until completely combined. Pour the wet ingredients into the well in the dry ingredients, mixing gently until almost combined. Fold in the berries until just incorporated, being careful not to overwork the batter (the batter should not be completely smooth; there should still be some visible lumps and bumps).

Scoop the batter into the prepared tins, filling the cups two-thirds full. Sprinkle the tops generously with the streusel. Bake 18 to 22 minutes, until the edges are golden brown and a wooden skewer or toothpick inserted in the center comes out with the tiniest bit of crumb.

NOTES: The berries do not have to be thawed, but the muffins may need an extra minute or two added to the baking time if frozen fruit is used.

Most fruit will work well in this recipe. Raspberries, strawberries, pears, peaches, rhubarb, peaches, cherries, and blackberries are all good options. For larger fruit (anything larger than a blueberry or raspberry), be sure to chop them into smaller diced pieces. You can also do a fruit/chocolate/nut combination here. I find 1½ cups fruit and ½ cup chocolate or nuts works best. Just be sure you don't add more than 2 cups total.

PUMPKIN-OLIVE OIL BREAD

I have vivid holiday memories of countertops lined with cookies and bars, candy and breads. My mom would spend many of our vacation days baking goodies for the neighborhood, sending my sister and me off Christmas Eve morning to deliver them. On our way we would fight over who got to hold the prettiest bundle, and at some point one of us would always fall on the snowy sidewalk. Every door swung open to reveal a smiling face, exclaiming delight at my mom's fresh-baked pumpkin bread, while handing us their sweet offerings of Christmas cheer. The recipe, minus the olive oil, is from our old church cookbook It's a loaf that I now share with neighbors on my own street. *makes two 8-inch loaves*

3 cups (426 g) all-purpose flour

1½ teaspoons ground cinnamon

¾ teaspoon ground ginger

½ teaspoon grated nutmeg

2 teaspoons baking soda

1 teaspoon salt

4 large eggs

1½ cups (297 g) granulated sugar

1½ cups (297 g) packed brown sugar

½ cup olive oil

8 tablespoons (113 g) unsalted butter, melted and cooled

2 teaspoons pure vanilla extract

One 15-ounce (425 g) can unsweetened pumpkin puree

1½ cups (171 g) pecan halves, toasted and chopped

Adjust an oven rack to the lower middle position. Preheat the oven to 350°F. Grease two 8 by 4-inch loaf pans and line each with a parchment sling (page 15).

In a medium bowl, whisk the flour, cinnamon, ginger, nutmeg, baking soda, and salt.

In the bowl of a stand mixer fitted with a paddle, beat the eggs on medium-high until pale yellow and doubled in size, 2 to 3 minutes. Add the granulated and brown sugars and beat on medium for 2 minutes. Add the oil, butter, vanilla, and pumpkin and mix on low until incorporated. Scrape down the sides of the bowl and add the flour mixture. Mix on low until combined and no lumps remain. Add the pecans and mix on low until just combined.

Divide the batter equally into the prepared pans and bake 50 to 60 minutes, until a wooden skewer or toothpick inserted in the center comes out clean. If the tops of the loaves brown too quickly, lay a piece of aluminum foil over them.

Transfer the pans to a wire rack and let cool for 20 minutes. Using the parchment sling, lift the loaves out of the pan, peel off the paper, and let the bread finish cooling on the wire rack.

BANANA BREAD

I know there are a million recipes for banana bread, all of them claiming to be the best. I've tried many different variations over the years, from those made with whole wheat flour and flaxseed to cakelike loaves that were chock-full of chocolate chips and peanut butter. They were all delicious. But there is one recipe that has traveled with me from coffeehouse to coffeehouse and is now a staple in our home. I've given it a few adjustments over the years, but it hasn't strayed much from the original recipe we made at the Blue Heron Coffeehouse.

I'm not going to lie. It's not on the healthful end of the spectrum, but it's rich and delicious, always moist, and full of banana flavor. And it's the best. *makes one 8-inch loaf*

1½ cups (213 g) all-purpose flour

1 teaspoon baking soda

1 teaspoon salt

½ cup (57 g) pecan halves, toasted and chopped

1 cup very ripe bananas, mashed (about 3 bananas)

½ cup sour cream

1 tablespoon pure vanilla extract

8 tablespoons (1 stick; 113 g) unsalted butter, room temperature

½ cup (99 g) granulated sugar

½ cup (99 g) packed brown sugar

2 large eggs, room temperature

Adjust an oven rack to the lower middle position. Preheat the oven to 350°F. Grease an 8 by 4-inch loaf pan and line with a parchment sling (page 15).

In a small bowl, whisk the flour, baking soda, salt, and pecans. In a medium bowl, mix the bananas, sour cream, and vanilla.

In the bowl of a stand mixer fitted with a paddle, beat the butter on medium until creamy. Add the granulated and brown sugars and beat on medium until light and fluffy, 2 to 3 minutes. Scrape down the sides of the bowl. Add the eggs and mix on medium until combined. Add the flour mixture and mix on low until almost incorporated. Add the banana mixture and mix on low until completely combined. Scrape down the sides of the bowl and finish mixing with a spatula until the batter is completely combined. Pour the batter into the prepared baking pan and bake 45 to 55 minutes, until the top is dark brown and a wooden skewer or toothpick inserted into the center comes out clean.

CONTINUED

Transfer the pan to a wire rack and let cool for 20 minutes. Using the parchment sling, lift the loaves out of the pan, peel off the paper, and let the bread finish cooling on the wire rack.

VARIATION

banana chocolate chip bread · Substitute ½ cup (85 g) chocolate chips for the pecans.

NOTE: The trick to giving your banana bread a great flavor is to use very ripe bananas—the blacker the better. I like to freeze my peeled, ripe bananas in a freezer bag, and then move them from the freezer to the fridge the night before baking. As the bananas thaw, they leak a lot of banana juice. I put all the juice in a saucepan and cook it down to ¼ cup (off heat, I'll occasionally add 1 tablespoon of bourbon as well). After it has cooled, I add it to the batter along with the bananas. It makes for a very flavorful loaf.

CHOCOLATE BREAD

❦

I made a version of this bread (or is it a cake?) for years at Bordertown Coffee; customers begged for it, but my baking staff always found it troublesome because the batter tended to leak over the sides of the pan onto the oven floor. After years of fiddling with elaborate parchment paper tents, it dawned on me that a Pullman pan would solve the problem—its tall sides would prevent the batter from overflowing. It indeed works like a charm.

The famous version of this sunken loaf is in Nigella Lawson's *How to Be a Domestic Goddess*. I've tinkered with the recipe here and there, adding a few more ounces of bittersweet chocolate, hot coffee, and salt for some complexity. The flavor of the chocolate is deeper and darker a day or two after the bread has been made, but a slice of this warm is quite a treat. Do what you have to do. *serves 6 to 8*

6 ounces (170 g) bittersweet chocolate

1½ cups (213 g) all-purpose flour

1 teaspoon baking soda

½ pound (2 sticks; 227 g) unsalted butter, room temperature

1½ cups (297 g) packed brown sugar

¾ teaspoon salt

2 large eggs

2 teaspoons pure vanilla extract

½ cup freshly brewed hot coffee

½ cup boiling water

Adjust an oven rack to the lower middle position. Preheat the oven to 375°F. Grease a 9 by 4 by 4-inch Pullman pan and line with a parchment paper sling (page 15), leaving an overhang on both sides.

Melt the chocolate in a heatproof bowl set over a pan of boiling water, being careful not to let the water touch the bottom of the bowl. Stir constantly until just melted and set aside to cool slightly.

In a small bowl, combine the flour and baking soda.

In the bowl of a stand mixer fitted with a paddle, beat the butter on medium until smooth. Add the sugar and salt and mix on medium until light and fluffy, 2 to 3 minutes. Add the eggs and vanilla and beat on medium until fully incorporated, scraping down the sides of the bowl as necessary. Add the chocolate and mix on low until incorporated, being careful not to overbeat. With the mixer on low add the flour,

CONTINUED

a tablespoon at a time, alternately with the boiling water and coffee (you can mix water and coffee together for simplicity), mixing until smooth and liquidy.

Pour the batter into the prepared pan and bake 30 minutes. Reduce the oven to 325°F and bake 15 minutes. The loaf will still be moist inside, so a wooden skewer or toothpick inserted into the center won't come out clean. But this is a good thing.

Transfer the pan to a wire rack and let cool before taking the bread out of the pan, using the parchment sling, and serving. The bread will sink a little in the middle as it cools.

NOTES: If you don't have a Pullman pan, you can use a standard 9-inch loaf pan. Be warned, however, that the batter has a tendency to leak over the sides as it's baking, and a parchment sling is essential for keeping the bread in the pan, as well as removing the bread from the pan. I put a baking sheet under the loaf pan before baking to catch any spills, just in case.

The sunken middle can be filled with all kinds of goodness (such as crème fraîche, whipped cream, or mixed berries), or you can serve the bread plain, which is my favorite way to partake of it.

LEMON BREAD

My breakfast of choice while working at the Blue Heron was a scone, hands down. But one rainy day we had a line out the door for hours, and by the time I finally got to sneak away to indulge in my morning ritual, there were no flaky triangles in sight. I did spy a lone piece of lemon bread in the bake case, and I halfheartedly put it on a plate and sat down. Lamenting that my routine had been disrupted, I took a bite. It was as if the sun had broken through all the haze of rain clouds; everything was brighter as the tart lemon glaze hit my tongue. Pablo Neruda describes the lemon as "a universe of gold, a yellow goblet of miracles." I'd have to agree and find this lemon bread to be my own little morning marvel. *serves 6 to 8*

1¾ cups (249 g) all-purpose flour

1½ teaspoons baking powder

¼ teaspoon baking soda

¾ teaspoon salt

¼ cup lemon juice

½ cup sour cream

8 tablespoons (1 stick; 113 g) unsalted butter, room temperature

1¼ cups (248 g) sugar

2 tablespoons grated lemon zest

2 large eggs, room temperature

2 tablespoons canola oil

½ teaspoon pure vanilla extract

LEMON GLAZE

¼ cup (50 g) sugar

¼ cup lemon juice

Pinch salt

Adjust the oven rack to the lower middle position. Preheat the oven to 350°F. Grease an 8 by 4-inch loaf pan and line with a parchment sling (page 15).

In a medium bowl, whisk the flour, baking powder, baking soda, and salt. In a small bowl, mix the lemon juice and sour cream.

In the bowl of a stand mixer fitted with a paddle, beat the butter on medium until smooth. Add the sugar and lemon zest and beat on medium until light and fluffy, 2 to 3 minutes. Add the eggs one at a time, beating well on medium after each addition and scraping down the sides as needed. Add the canola oil and vanilla and mix on low until combined. Add half the flour mixture and mix on low until almost combined. Add the sour cream mixture and mix on low to incorporate. Add the remaining flour mixture and mix on low until completely combined.

CONTINUED

Pour the batter into the prepared pan and bake 45 to 60 minutes, until a wooden skewer or toothpick inserted in the center comes out clean.

Transfer the pan to a wire rack and let cool for 20 minutes. While the bread is cooling in the pan, make the lemon glaze. Using the parchment sling, lift the loaf out of the pan, and peel off the paper. Brush the top and sides of the warm bread with the lemon glaze. Then let the bread finish cooling on the wire rack before slicing.

FOR THE GLAZE: Combine the sugar, lemon juice, and salt in a small saucepan. Boil gently over medium heat until a light syrup forms and the liquid reduces slightly, 6 to 8 minutes.

GINGER-CHOCOLATE BREAD

Colleen introduced me to the combination of ginger and chocolate at the Blue Heron, and while I first thought it highly unusual, I've grown to love the pairing. She often used the two together in scones or muffins, but I've re-created her magic here in loaf form, with a good amount of chocolate and a double dose of ginger: fresh and ground. Swirling chocolate into the batter and then topping the loaf again with it after it has cooled makes for a rich and spicy bite and a beautiful presentation. ***serves 6 to 8***

2 ounces (57 g) bittersweet chocolate, melted and cooled

1½ cups (213 g) all-purpose flour

½ teaspoon baking powder

1 teaspoon baking soda

½ teaspoon salt

1½ teaspoons ground ginger

8 tablespoons (1 stick; 113 g) unsalted butter, room temperature

1 cup (198 g) sugar

1 tablespoon grated fresh gingerroot

2 large eggs, room temperature

2 tablespoons canola oil

1 teaspoon pure vanilla extract

¼ cup sour cream

½ cup whole milk

2 ounces (57 g) bittersweet chocolate, melted and cooled, for topping

Adjust an oven rack to the lower middle position. Preheat the oven to 350°F. Grease an 8 by 4-inch loaf pan and line with a parchment sling (page 15).

Put about 1 inch of water in a medium saucepan and bring it to a gentle boil.

Melt 2 ounces of the chocolate in a heatproof bowl set over the pan of boiling water, being careful not to let the water touch the bottom of the bowl. Stir constantly until just melted and set aside to cool slightly.

In a medium bowl, whisk the flour, baking powder, baking soda, salt, and ground ginger.

In the bowl of a stand mixer fitted with a paddle, beat the butter on medium until smooth. Add the sugar and grated ginger and beat on medium until light and fluffy, 2 to 3 minutes. Add the eggs one at a time, beating on medium after each addition to incorporate and scraping down the sides of the bowl as needed. Add the canola oil and vanilla and mix on low to combine. Add one-third of the flour mixture to the bowl and beat on low to combine. Add the sour cream and beat on low to incorporate. Add half

CONTINUED

of the remaining flour mixture, and then the milk, beating on low after each addition to incorporate. Add the remaining flour and mix on low until just combined.

Transfer ½ cup of the batter to a medium bowl and add the 2 ounces of melted and cooled chocolate. Stir until completely combined.

Scrape the white batter into the prepared pan. Drop the chocolate batter in circles over the top and, using a table knife, gently swirl it into the batter using a figure-eight motion. Try not to drag the chocolate to the bottom or edges of the pan.

Bake 45 to 60 minutes, until a wooden skewer or toothpick inserted in the center comes out clean.

Transfer the pan to a wire rack and let cool 15 minutes. Using the parchment sling, lift the loaf out of the pan, peel off the paper, and let the bread finish cooling on the wire rack. Top the cooled loaf with the remaining 2 ounces of melted chocolate, smoothing it out with an offset spatula or table knife. Let the chocolate set and harden before slicing.

NOTE: For extra ginger flavor, add ¼ cup chopped crystallized ginger to the white batter and mix to combine.

PUMPKIN POUND CAKE WITH CHOCOLATE

This is another recipe that has been with me through several baking gigs. Originally it appeared in a café I worked at in Minneapolis and was a customer favorite each and every time it found its way into the bake case. I took the recipe with me to Bordertown Coffee, and it was lauded as a beloved breakfast there. The recipe is actually similar to the Pumpkin–Olive Oil Bread (page 89) and most likely came out of a church cookbook of some sort as well. I love the combination of pumpkin and chocolate here, but they could be replaced with pecans or dried cherries. *serves 8 to 12*

3 cups (426 g) all-purpose flour

2 teaspoons baking soda

1 teaspoon salt

1½ teaspoons ground cinnamon

¾ teaspoon ground ginger

½ teaspoon grated nutmeg

4 large eggs

1½ cups (297 g) granulated sugar

1½ cups (297 g) packed brown sugar

¾ cup canola oil

One 15-ounce (425 g) can unsweetened pumpkin puree

2 teaspoons pure vanilla extract

8 ounces (226 g) bittersweet chocolate, chopped

Confectioners' sugar for dusting

Adjust an oven rack to the lower middle position. Preheat the oven to 350°F. Grease and flour a 10-inch tube or Bundt pan.

In a large bowl, whisk the flour, baking soda, salt, cinnamon, ginger, and nutmeg.

In a stand mixer fitted with a paddle, beat the eggs on medium until pale yellow and doubled in volume, 4 to 5 minutes. Add the granulated and brown sugars and mix on medium until well combined. Add the oil, pumpkin, and vanilla and mix on medium again until completely combined. Add the flour mixture and mix on medium until smooth. Stir in the chocolate with a spatula.

Pour the batter into the prepared pan and bake 45 to 60 minutes, until a wooden skewer or toothpick inserted in the center comes out clean.

Transfer the pan to a wire rack and let cool for 20 minutes. Invert the cake onto the rack to finish cooling. Dust with confectioners' sugar before slicing.

HONEY BUNDT CAKE

Throughout my reading experience, I've come across references to honey cakes more than once. Everyone from the inhabitants of Middle-earth to the prophets of the Old Testament mention this thick, sticky liquid at some point. In my mind, these amber cakes conjure up images of countryside picnics with the Bennet sisters and stumbling around J. R. R. Tolkien's Middle-earth only discover Beorn's house and his table laden with delicacies. After escaping in books for an entire afternoon, I headed to the kitchen to create my own golden circles, hoping to capture the taste that was held dear in so many literary moments. A moist honey cake topped with even more honey in frosting form was the last chapter. *serves 8 to 12*

3 cups (426 g) all-purpose flour

2 teaspoons baking powder

1 teaspoon salt

¾ teaspoon ground cinnamon

¼ teaspoon grated nutmeg

¾ pound (3 sticks; 339 g) unsalted butter, room temperature

1½ cups (297 g) granulated sugar

¼ cup (50 g) packed brown sugar

1 cup honey

5 large eggs, room temperature

1 teaspoon pure vanilla extract

2 teaspoons lemon juice

1 cup buttermilk

HONEY FROSTING

3 ounces (86 g) cream cheese, room temperature

5 tablespoons (74 g) unsalted butter, room temperature

¼ cup honey

½ teaspoon pure vanilla extract

Pinch salt

1 cup (113 g) confectioners' sugar

Adjust the oven rack to the lower middle position. Preheat the oven to 325°F. Grease and flour a 10-inch tube or Bundt pan.

In a medium bowl, whisk the flour, baking powder, salt, cinnamon, and nutmeg.

In the bowl of a stand mixer fitted with a paddle, beat the butter on medium until smooth. Add the granulated and brown sugars and beat on medium until light and fluffy, 3 to 5 minutes. Add the honey and mix on medium until smooth. Add the eggs, one at a time and beat on medium until incorporated, stopping to scrape down the sides of the bowl after each addition. Add the vanilla and lemon juice and mix on low to combine. Add the flour mixture and mix on low until just combined. Slowly add the buttermilk and mix on low until just combined.

CONTINUED

Pour the batter into the prepared pan and use a spatula to even out the top. Bake 60 to 75 minutes, until a wooden skewer or toothpick inserted in the center comes out clean.

Transfer the pan to a wire rack and let cool for 20 minutes. Remove the cake from the pan and let finish cooling on the rack. Top the cooled cake with the Honey Frosting.

FOR THE HONEY FROSTING: In the bowl of a stand mixer fitted with a paddle, beat the cream cheese and butter on medium until smooth. Add the honey, vanilla, and salt and mix on low until combined. Add the confectioners' sugar and beat on low until combined, then increase the speed to medium and beat until the frosting is light and fluffy, 3 to 5 minutes.

CREAMY ALMOND COFFEE CAKE

Coffee cake filled with cream cheese and topped with sugar and nuts has always been on my list of breakfast favorites. However, it turned out to be rather difficult to get this type of cake just right. I started with a recipe I had clipped from a magazine years ago, but I felt it needed some adjusting. I got the base and flavor exactly how I wanted it, but twenty-five cakes later I still had a cream cheese filling with gaping holes and no zing. Finally, my tweaks were perfected, thanks to a few tips I found online. The cake needed just a squeeze of lemon and a good bang or two on the counter, then everything came together: a moist crumb, a subtle almond flavor, and a cream cheese swirl to knock it all out of the park. *serves 8 to 12*

2¾ cups (391 g) all-purpose flour

1¼ cups (248 g) sugar

2 teaspoons grated lemon zest

1¼ teaspoons salt

14 tablespoons (1¾ sticks; 199 g) unsalted butter, room temperature

¾ cup (65 g) sliced almonds

1 teaspoon baking powder

1 teaspoon baking soda

¾ cup whole milk

¾ cup sour cream

4 large eggs

1 teaspoon pure vanilla extract

½ teaspoon almond extract

CREAM CHEESE FILLING

8 ounces (226 g) cream cheese, room temperature

⅓ cup (66 g) sugar

1 tablespoon lemon juice

½ teaspoon pure vanilla extract

Adjust the oven rack to the lower middle position. Preheat the oven to 350°F. Grease a 10-inch tube pan.

FOR THE COFFEE CAKE: In the bowl of a stand mixer fitted with a paddle, mix the flour, sugar, lemon zest, and salt on low. Add the butter and mix on medium until the mixture resembles coarse sand. Transfer 1 cup of the flour mixture to a small bowl, stir in the almonds, and set aside.

Add the baking powder and baking soda to the stand mixer bowl. Mix on low to incorporate into the remaining flour mixture. In a medium bowl or liquid measuring cup, combine the milk, sour cream, eggs, vanilla, and almond extract. Pour the liquid

CONTINUED

ingredients into the dry and mix on medium to combine, beating until the batter is almost smooth, 20 to 30 seconds. Transfer all but about 2 tablespoons of the batter to a large bowl. Set aside.

FOR THE CREAM CHEESE FILLING: Put the cream cheese into the mixing bowl with the 2 tablespoons of batter and beat on medium until smooth, 1 to 2 minutes. Scrape down the sides of the bowl and add the sugar, lemon juice, and vanilla. Mix on low until combined and then beat on medium until smooth and creamy.

FOR BAKING: Pour half the batter into the prepared pan and smooth the top. Scoop the cream cheese filling on top of the batter, distributing it evenly and doing your best to keep it away from the edges of the pan. Use a knife or offset spatula to even out the top. Cover the cream cheese filling evenly with the remaining batter and smooth out the top again. Use a knife or offset spatula to gently swirl the cream cheese into the batter using a figure-eight motion, trying not to drag the filling to the bottom or edges of the pan. Sprinkle the reserved flour-almond mixture evenly over the batter and press the topping down gently. Give the pan a few sharp taps on the counter.

Bake 45 to 55 minutes, until the top is golden and firm and a wooden skewer or toothpick inserted in the center comes out clean. (Note that the toothpick will be wet if it is inserted directly into the cream cheese.)

Remove the pan from the oven and give it another three or four taps on a heatproof surface. The cake will sink a bit, but this will ensure there are no large holes in the cream cheese filling.

Transfer the pan to a wire rack and let cool for at least 1 hour before removing it from the pan. Invert the cake on a plate or baking sheet, remove the tube pan, and then invert the cake topping side up onto a wire rack to finish cooling. Let cool to room temperature before serving.

BLACKBERRY-POPPY SEED BUTTERMILK CAKE

There is something about the phrase *everyday cake* that is downright charming, calling to mind Jane Austen novels and seedcakes made in J. R. R. Tolkien's Middle-earth. This particular cake is, in fact, good enough for any day. Buttermilk, almond, blackberries, and poppy seeds all make for a delicious, well-rounded bite. *serves 6 to 8*

"If more of us valued food and cheer and song above hoarded gold, it would be a merrier world." —J.R.R. TOLKIEN

1½ cups (213 g) all-purpose flour

¾ teaspoon baking powder

½ teaspoon baking soda

¾ teaspoon salt

1½ teaspoons poppy seeds

8 tablespoons (1 stick; 113 g) unsalted butter, room temperature

1 cup (198 g) sugar, plus 1 tablespoon for sprinkling

1 large egg

1 teaspoon pure vanilla extract

½ teaspoon almond extract

1 cup buttermilk

1¼ cups (213 g) blackberries, coarsely chopped into bite-sized picees

Adjust the oven rack to the lower middle position. Preheat the oven to 350°F. Grease and flour a 9 by 2-inch round cake pan and line the bottom with parchment paper.

In a medium bowl, whisk the flour, baking powder, baking soda, salt, and poppy seeds.

In the bowl of a stand mixer fitted with a paddle, beat the butter on medium until smooth. Add the sugar and beat on medium until light and fluffy, 3 to 5 minutes. Add the egg and beat on medium until combined. Add the vanilla and almond extracts and beat on low until incorporated. Add half the flour mixture and mix on low until just combined. With the mixer running on low, add the buttermilk in a slow, steady stream; stop the mixer and scrape down the sides of the bowl. Add the rest of the flour and mix on low until just combined. Add the blackberries and stir gently with a spatula until they are just mixed in.

Pour the batter into the prepared pan. Smooth the top with an offset spatula or table knife and sprinkle the top with the remaining tablespoon of sugar. Bake 25 to 32 minutes, until the cake is golden and a wooden skewer or toothpick inserted in the center comes out with the tiniest bit of crumb.

Transfer the pan to a wire rack and let cool for 15 minutes. Remove the cake from the pan and finish cooling on the rack.

ORANGE-CRANBERRY BUNDT CAKE

Everyone needs a recipe for a good, all-purpose Bundt cake. I've made it here with orange and cranberries, but there is much room for your own interpretation. You can substitute any other small berry for the cranberries, and lemon for the orange. It's perfect for a casual morning get-together, an elegant brunch, or afternoon snacking all by your lonesome. I make the cake the evening before serving to let the flavors fully develop. *makes 8 to 12 servings*

3 cups (426 g) all-purpose flour

1 teaspoon baking powder

¾ teaspoon salt

¾ pound (3 sticks, 226 g) unsalted butter, room temperature

2¼ cups (446 g) sugar

1 tablespoon grated orange zest

5 large eggs, room temperature

2 teaspoons pure vanilla extract

1 tablespoon Grand Marnier or other orange liqueur

¼ cup orange juice

1 tablespoon lemon juice

¼ cup heavy cream

2 heaping cups (227 g) cranberries, fresh or frozen

Confectioners' Sugar Glaze (page 311)

Adjust the oven rack to the lower middle position. Preheat the oven to 325°F. Grease a 10-inch tube pan or Bundt pan.

In a medium bowl, mix together the flour, baking powder, and salt.

In the bowl of a stand mixer fitted with a paddle, beat the butter on medium speed until creamy. Add the sugar and orange zest, and beat together on medium until light and fluffy, 2 to 3 minutes. Add the eggs one at a time, beating well after each addition, stopping to scrape down the sides of the bowl as needed. Add the vanilla and Grand Marnier and mix on low to combine. Add one-third of the flour mixture and mix on low to combine. Add the orange juice and lemon juice and mix on low to combine. Add half the remaining flour and then the heavy cream, beating on low after each addition to incorporate. Add the remaining flour and mix on low until just combined. Add the cranberries and stir with a spatula to combine.

Pour the batter into the prepared pan and bake 60 to 75 minutes, until a wooden skewer or toothpick inserted into the center comes out with the slightest bit of crumb.

Transfer the pan to a wire rack and let cool for 25 minutes. Remove the cake from the pan and cool completely on a wire rack. Top the cooled cake with the Confectioners' Sugar Glaze and let set before slicing.

PICNIC CAKES

Picnic cakes are small, simple treats that can be wrapped up and slipped into a backpack or picnic basket and are perfect for nibbling on and sharing with other wanderers. They are inspired by the many cake references in Tolkien's books—my heart always flutters at Bilbo's larder full of cakes and pies and apple tarts. These cakes are modest, with a subtle almond flavor and tender crumb. My daughter, son, and I like to each wrap one in parchment paper to carry into the woods that border our backyard. We find a tucked away spot to unfurl our blanket, and there we quietly sit, looking for elves and hobbits while snacking on our sweet little circles. *makes three 6-inch cakes*

1½ cups (213 g) all-purpose flour

¾ teaspoon baking powder

½ teaspoon baking soda

¾ teaspoon salt

8 tablespoons (1 stick; 113 g) unsalted butter, room temperature

1 cup (198 g) sugar, plus 2 tablespoons for sprinkling

2 large eggs

1 teaspoon pure vanilla extract

¾ teaspoon almond extract

½ cup buttermilk

½ cup sour cream

1 cup (100 g) sliced almonds

Adjust the oven rack to the lower middle position. Preheat the oven to 375°F. Grease and flour three 6 by 2-inch round cake pans and line the bottoms with parchment paper.

In a medium bowl, whisk the flour, baking powder, baking soda, and salt.

In the bowl of a stand mixer fitted with a paddle, beat the butter on medium until smooth. Add the sugar and beat until light and fluffy, 2 to 3 minutes. Add the eggs and beat on medium until combined. Add the vanilla extract and almond extract and beat on low until combined. Add half the flour mixture and mix on low until just combined. With the mixer running on low, add the buttermilk in a slow steady stream; stop the mixer and scrape down the sides of the bowl. Add the sour cream and mix on low until combined. Add the rest of the flour mixture and beat on low until just combined.

Pour the batter evenly into the prepared pans. Smooth the tops with an offset spatula or table knife, then sprinkle each evenly with the almonds and the remaining 2 tablespoons of sugar. Bake 18 to 22 minutes, until golden and a wooden skewer or toothpick comes out clean.

Transfer the pans to a wire rack and let cool for 15 minutes. Remove the cakes from the pans and finish cooling on the wire rack.

chapter three

PARTY CAKES

Throughout my preteen years, I spent a good part of each summer vacation tucked away in my bedroom, eagerly devouring Nancy Drew mysteries. While I enjoyed all the suspense and excitement of the novels, I also picked up quite a few important life lessons from Ms. Drew that have stayed with me all these years. First, I learned to always keep a packed suitcase in the trunk of my car with every possible type of clothing in it; swimsuits and snow pants may be needed in an emergency. I know to have a tube of red lipstick in my purse at all times, as it can be used for many things, including writing help notes on the window of the airplane one is currently kidnapped in. But most important, I learned never to trust anyone who is both handsome and charming. Either he will be completely shallow and just get in the way of solving the crime or else he'll turn out to be the thief who started the whole mystery (and I will end up trying to outrun him in a pencil skirt and heels).

Sadly, most party cakes are like that handsome charmer—meticulously dressed and smooth as silk—but one doesn't need a magnifying glass to see what's really lurking underneath: nothing but disappointing flavor and a bunch of dry crumbs. I spent a good amount of time solving the puzzle of how to make quality cakes that wouldn't disappoint, cakes that would be consistent, faithful friends in the years to come. Chocolate, vanilla, and white cake are the bases used throughout this chapter, along with many varieties of buttercream to mix and match to your heart's content. And while I never expected to use Nancy's mystery-solving advice in the kitchen, I'm happy to see those hours spent reading didn't go to waste.

ON BAKING CAKES

The three main cake recipes in this chapter (chocolate, yellow, and white) will work best when baked in two 8 by 2-inch round cake pans. You can also use 9 by 2-inch pans, but you will need to take a few minutes off the baking time, and the cakes will be a little flatter. You can also use three cake pans, which will give you lighter layers and an extremely tall finished cake. You'll also have to take 5 to 7 minutes off the baking time if you use three pans. You'll know the cakes are done when the cake begins to pull away from the sides of the pan, and the tiniest bit of crumb is on a wooden skewer or toothpick inserted into the middle. Each recipe gives specific baking times for baking the cakes in two pans unless noted.

ON FROSTING CAKES

Make sure the cakes are completely cool before you frost them. I like to put my layers in the freezer for 15 to 20 minutes to chill them before frosting; I've found this helps the buttercream go on much smoother and helps the crumbs stay put.

    If your layers have a large dome, you can slice off the rounded bump for a straight top if desired. This will help make your cake look even and professional. I also cool my cakes top side down (the bump on top touching the wire rack) and have found this helps deflate the dome. If your cake is a little lopsided, applying the buttercream will even out any dents or lumps.

Frosting Your Cake on a Turntable

Arrange your first layer, cut side up on the turntable. If your layers aren't cut, put the first layer top side up. A cardboard cutout (see page 31) is a helpful tool for moving the cake to and from the refrigerator, and I highly recommend using one. You can set a damp paper towel underneath the cutout so it doesn't slide around. Keep a pastry brush nearby and brush off any loose crumbs during the frosting process.

    Place buttercream on the first layer. If the recipe specifies how much buttercream, use that amount; otherwise I place about 1 cup of frosting between each layer. Use an offset spatula or butter knife to spread the frosting evenly over the layer, all the way to the edges.

    Top the buttercream with the second layer of cake, cut side down. If your cake layers aren't cut, put the flattest side of the cake up. If your cake has more than two layers, repeat the previous steps for frosting layers.

APPLY A CRUMB COAT · Make sure your cake layers are even; you want them to line up together, and none of them should be sticking out farther than the others. Gently press to adjust them if you need to and use a ruler or straightedge to make sure they are lined up evenly. With an offset spatula, apply a thin, even layer of buttercream to the top and the sides of the cake, covering every surface, and filling in the gaps between layers. Smooth out any bumps or lumps in the thin coat. Be careful if you need to apply more buttercream to not get crumbs from the spatula back into your mixing bowl. Move the cake into the freezer or refrigerator to chill the cake and harden the buttercream. This will keep the crumbs in place, locking them into the crumb coat. I put my cake on a baking sheet and put it in the freezer for 10 minutes to chill, but if you don't have room, place it in the refrigerator for 20 minutes.

APPLY A FINISHING COAT · Take the cake from the freezer or refrigerator and put it back in the center of the turntable, with another damp paper towel underneath the cardboard cutout. Place a large amount of buttercream on the top of the cake. With an offset spatula, smooth the buttercream on the top of the cake, so it is a perfectly level layer (this will cover up any unevenness as well). When the top is even, move on to the sides. Put a good amount of buttercream onto the spatula and then use the spatula to put the buttercream on the sides of the cake in a thick layer. Don't worry about getting it perfectly smooth at this point, just make sure you have a nice thick coat, covering all the cake. Press the spatula very gently against the cake at a slight angle and move the turntable in a constant, fluid circle. As the table moves, the spatula will begin to collect some of the excess buttercream and even out the sides. Stop to clean the spatula off a few times. You want to be careful not to take too much of the buttercream off, or you will start to see the cake layers underneath. Keep turning the table until the buttercream is as smooth and even as possible. A slight edge will have built up on the top of the cake and with your spatula at an angle, run it across the top to even it out.

FINISH DECORATING · The cake will be smooth at this point. You can leave it as is, or add some more decoration to it. When finished decorating, move the cake to a cake stand to serve.

Frosting Your Cake on a Cake Stand

If you are frosting the cake directly on a serving plate, you will not need a cardboard cutout. Place a small amount of buttercream (about a heaping tablespoon) in the center of the cake stand and then place the first cake layer on top of the frosting. This will help keep your cake from sliding around. Place a few small pieces of parchment paper underneath the edges of the cake. I cut three or four pieces in a rectangular shape and overlap them underneath the edges of the cake; any buttercream that spills will fall onto the parchment, and the cake stand will stay clean.

Apply a crumb coat (detailed above), but instead of spinning a turntable, you will gently move the cake stand as needed to cover the entire cake in a thin layer of buttercream. Move the cake and stand to your refrigerator and chill for 20 minutes.

When the cake is chilled and firm, place a large amount of frosting on the top of the cake. With an offset spatula, smooth the frosting on the top of the cake, so it is a perfectly level layer (this will cover up any unevenness as well). When the top is even, move to the sides. Put some of the buttercream onto the spatula, and then use the spatula to put the buttercream on the sides of the cake in a thick layer. Don't worry about getting it perfectly smooth at this point, just make sure you have a nice thick coat, covering all the cake. Smooth out the buttercream in an even layer, and then decorate as desired. Remove the parchment paper underneath the cake before serving.

ON DECORATING CAKES

In all honesty, I prefer a stripped-down cake over one with lots of bells and whistles. I try to keep my decorating to a minimum and look around for simple ideas to slightly embellish. Here are a few easy ways to adorn your party cake.

FLOWERS · Fresh flowers are a beautiful and easy way to decorate your cake. I like to keep the sides very smooth and top the cake with large, colorful blooms. Make sure to use flowers that have not been sprayed with pesticides.

HORIZONTAL STRIPES · Rest the tip of an offset spatula against the bottom of your iced cake. Gently spin the turntable and slowly begin to move the spatula up as the table spins, to create lines around the cake. Keep rotating and moving the spatula up the sides of the cake until you reach the top. This won't work as well without a turntable, but you can move the spatula around the cake to get a similar effect.

TEXTURE · Press the edge of an icing comb gently against your iced cake. Spin your turntable and run the comb around your cake to form ridges. Turn the table until the comb has gone all the way around the cake. Without a turntable, you can carefully move the icing comb around the cake.

SPRINKLES/NUTS · Sprinkles are a fun and easy way to add color to your cake. If you are having trouble with frosting your cake, if you didn't use a crumb coat and there are crumbs in the buttercream, or if you just can't get the sides smooth, sprinkles or chopped nuts can hide mistakes. Gently press them up against the sides of the cake until the entire side of the cake is covered. The top can be left plain, or also covered.

TYPES OF BUTTERCREAM/FROSTING

There are several varieties of buttercream to choose from when icing a cake. This chapter focuses on four different types: Swiss Meringue, Italian Meringue, American, and Flour Buttercream. Buttercream is also often called frosting or icing, but for ease I've referred to it as buttercream through this chapter.

SWISS MERINGUE BUTTERCREAM · Egg whites and sugar are heated gently over a double boiler, then whipped until voluminous. Butter is added, pieces at a time, and then whipped again until silky smooth. See Swiss Meringue Buttercream (page 126) and Mint Chocolate Cake (page 151).

ITALIAN MERINGUE BUTTERCREAM · Italian Meringue Buttercream is similar to Swiss Meringue, but instead of heating the whites and sugar together over a double boiler, hot sugar syrup is poured over the egg whites and then whipped. See Burnt Honey Buttercream (page 145).

AMERICAN BUTTERCREAM · Often seen on grocery store cakes, American buttercream is a quick and easy version that is usually made with shortening and piles of confectioners' sugar. It has a reputation for being sickly sweet, and many pastry chefs refuse to acknowledge it as buttercream, as most versions of it don't even contain butter. I've discovered that when it is made with butter, the confectioners' sugar is reduced, and when a good pinch of salt is added, it can be a delicious alternative to the time-consuming Swiss Meringue. See American Buttercream (page 125), Cardamom Cake with Coffee Buttercream (page 141), and Vanilla Cupcakes with Brown Butter Buttercream (page 161).

ERMINE BUTTERCREAM, OR FLOUR BUTTERCREAM · This buttercream is made by combining flour, sugar, salt, and milk together in a saucepan and then cooking it until a thick paste forms. Butter is then beaten into the cooled mixture. See Chocolate Ganache Cupcakes with Basil Buttercream (page 165).

SWISS MERINGUE BUTTERCREAM

Everything I know about buttercream I learned from Zoë François, either from hanging out in her kitchen and watching her decorate cakes in person or from devouring her website for tips and tricks. She's a genius, a pastry chef extraordinaire, and I am lucky to be able to learn her magic.

This is a basic vanilla Swiss meringue buttercream. It shows up in other flavors throughout the chapter, and I've added some variations so you can mix and match frosting and cakes as you see fit. *makes 6 cups*

8 large egg whites
2¼ cups (446 g) sugar
¼ teaspoon salt

1½ pounds (6 sticks; 678 g) unsalted butter, room temperature
1 vanilla bean, seeds scraped
2 teaspoons pure vanilla extract

Put about an inch of water in a medium saucepan and bring it to a gentle boil.

In the bowl of a stand mixer, stir the egg whites, sugar, and salt until combined. Place the bowl over the saucepan, being careful not to let the water touch the bottom of the bowl. Stir with a rubber spatula until the sugar is completely melted and reaches a temperature of 160°F, 4 to 5 minutes. While you are stirring, be sure to scrape down the sides of the bowl with the spatula—this will ensure no sugar grains are lurking on the sides and will help prevent the egg whites from cooking.

Remove the bowl from the heat and place it in the stand mixer fitted with a whisk. Whisk on medium-high speed until stiff, glossy peaks form, 8 to 10 minutes. The bowl should have cooled down to room temperature at this point. Reduce the speed to low and, with the mixer running, add 1 to 2 tablespoons of butter at a time (see notes), beating well after each addition. When the butter has been completely incorporated, add the vanilla bean seeds and vanilla extract. Beat on low until incorporated, then use immediately or cover and refrigerate for up to 1 week. When ready to use, let the buttercream come to room temperature and then beat again with a stand mixer until smooth. You can also freeze buttercream up to 2 months. Transfer the buttercream from the freezer to the refrigerator the night before needed; the next day let it come to room temperature and beat again with a stand mixer until smooth.

chocolate buttercream · Add 8 ounces melted and cooled bittersweet chocolate with the vanilla extract. Beat until just combined. The frosting will look very light, but will still have good chocolate flavor.

brown sugar · Replace the granulated sugar in the recipe with brown sugar.

peanut butter · Add 2 cups creamy peanut butter with the vanilla extract. Beat until well combined. This buttercream will be a bit softer due to the peanut butter, and won't pipe as easily. You can chill it for 10 to 15 minutes before decorating to help firm it up.

caramel · Add 1½ cups caramel, at room temperature, with the vanilla extract. Beat until well combined.

NOTES: At any point, the buttercream may look curdled and runny, but this is normal. Keep adding the rest of the butter, and as you beat the buttercream it will turn smooth and beautiful.

If, for some reason, the buttercream is still runny after beating, it may be that your butter or egg whites are too warm. Place the mixer bowl in the refrigerator for about 10 minutes, stirring the buttercream every couple minutes. Then beat again until smooth.

The butter needs to be added slowly to help it emulsify correctly into the meringue. Butter should be soft but cool when added, about 70°F. It should be soft enough to mix well, but firm enough to give some structure to the buttercream.

AMERICAN BUTTERCREAM

While I love Swiss Meringue Buttercream, sometimes there just isn't enough time to make it. This faster version of buttercream is a good substitute; it's still buttery and creamy, but without all the effort. *makes about 4 cups*

1 pound (4 sticks; 452 g) unsalted
butter, room temperature

2 teaspoons pure vanilla extract

¼ teaspoon salt

3 cups (339 g) confectioners' sugar

Food coloring (optional)

In the bowl of a stand mixer fitted with a paddle, beat the butter on medium until creamy. Scrape down the sides and add the vanilla and salt. Mix on low until combined and then beat on medium for 1 minute. Turn the mixer to low and slowly add the confectioners' sugar, a little at a time, mixing until combined, and stopping to scrape down the sides of the bowl as necessary. Add a few drops of food coloring, if desired, and mix on low until it is completely incorporated. Increase the speed to medium-high and beat 6 to 8 minutes until light and fluffy.

VARIATIONS

blood orange buttercream · Add 1 teaspoon blood orange zest, ¼ cup blood orange juice, and 2 tablespoons of triple sec along with the vanilla extract.

cream cheese buttercream · Reduce the butter to ¾ pound (3 sticks; 339 g) unsalted butter and 6 ounces (171 g) cream cheese at room temperature. Follow the recipe as directed.

lemon buttercream · Add 2 teaspoons lemon zest and ¼ cup lemon juice along with the vanilla extract.

NOTE: You can double this recipe easily if you need more buttercream for piping and decorating.

CHOCOLATE CAKE

Part of the reason I started *The Vanilla Bean Blog* revolved around chocolate cake. I was interested in creating some kind of family food history, an idea sparked when I realized my family did not have a cake to call our own. We bought cake and occasionally made cake, but no one ever requested a specific cake for birthdays, and there wasn't one particular recipe that made us swoon. I decided that needed to change.

I made chocolate cake after chocolate cake, only to come up with some not-so-great confections. Often they turned out dry or were missing that deep, dreamy chocolate flavor I was after. Eventually, however, I stumbled on black magic cake. Black magic cake has a history of its own; it's a Hershey's original, developed sometime before the 1970s and used as a label recipe in 1972. There are claims that the recipe goes back to possibly the 1930s, but no one knows the exact date of its creation; not even the Hershey Company could tell me when I reached out to them. All the usual cake ingredient suspects are there: sugar, flour, eggs, cocoa powder, vanilla, and oil, but what makes this recipe unique is at the end of mixing, one cup of hot coffee is added to the bowl. As the coffee is gently stirred in, the batter turns into an unpromising dark sludge, but bakes up into a moist, delicious cake.

Over the years, I discovered two things about black magic cake. One, the cake had made the rounds: many cookbooks and almost every website has some version in its pages; often hot water replaces the coffee (I even found a variation substituting tomato soup) and milk is used instead of buttermilk. Two, I wanted this cake to have more chocolate flavor. Topped with chocolate buttercream, it was indeed perfect, but paired with any other kind of frosting, I found it lacking. So I started testing, melting bittersweet chocolate and adding different amounts to the cake until I was pleased with the flavor. I added a little more flour as well; the cake constantly shed crumbs, and the extra flour helped. I liked my changes, but the cake was the tiniest bit too dry. One night, when I was up late once again making cakes, I accidently cracked an extra egg into the batter. When the cake baked up, it was exactly as I dreamed it should be: moist and tender, with perfect chocolate flavor. I tried it with various other frostings and it held its own. I finally had my family cake. *makes two 8-inch cakes*

CONTINUED

3 ounces (85 grams) bittersweet
  chocolate

1 cup freshly brewed coffee, hot

1 cup buttermilk

½ cup canola oil

3 large eggs, room temperature

2 teaspoons pure vanilla extract

2 cups (284 g) all-purpose flour

2 cups (396 g) sugar

¾ cup (75 g) Dutch process cocoa
  powder

2 teaspoons baking soda

1 teaspoon baking powder

1 teaspoon salt

Adjust an oven rack to the middle position. Preheat the oven to 350°F. Butter and flour two 8 by 2-inch round cake pans and line the bottoms with parchment paper.

Put the bittersweet chocolate in a small bowl. Pour the coffee over it and cover with a piece of plastic wrap. In a medium bowl or liquid measuring cup, whisk the buttermilk, canola oil, eggs, and vanilla.

In the bowl of a stand mixer fitted with a paddle, mix the flour, sugar, cocoa powder, baking soda, baking powder, and salt on low until combined. (If the cocoa powder is lumpy, you can sift it into the other ingredients.) With the mixer running on low, slowly add the buttermilk mixture. Increase the speed to medium and beat until combined, 20 to 30 seconds.

Whisk the chocolate and coffee together until completely smooth. With the mixer running on low, slowly pour the coffee mixture into the batter and mix until just combined. Using a spatula, give the batter a couple of turns to make sure it is fully mixed.

Pour the batter evenly into the prepared pans. Bake 25 to 35 minutes, until a wooden skewer or toothpick comes out with the tiniest bit of crumb.

Transfer the cakes to a wire rack and let cool for 30 minutes. Turn the cakes out onto the rack, remove the parchment paper, and let cool completely. Once cool, the cakes can be wrapped in plastic and refrigerated overnight or frosted.

VARIATION

chocolate–olive oil cake · Replace the canola oil with a good olive oil.

NOTES: This recipe will also work with 9 by 2-inch round cake pans and can be baked in three pans; for details and baking times, see page 120.

You can substitute hot water for the hot coffee, but the overall chocolate flavor will lack some depth.

YELLOW CAKE

{vanilla cake}

When I first began working on a yellow cake recipe, a few things were important to me. The cake needed to be buttery, full of vanilla flavor, and have a tender but sturdy crumb. I actually started with an old Bundt cake recipe I had and loved, adding vanilla, more salt, and a few eggs yolks to it. The taste was perfect, but the texture was just too fluffy for my liking. A reader suggested using the "reverse creaming" method, where butter is introduced to the dry ingredients instead of creamed with the sugars. It worked like a charm. I had a cake with a sturdy base and the delicate crumb I was after. *makes two 8-inch cakes*

3 large eggs

2 egg yolks

1 tablespoon pure vanilla extract

¾ cup sour cream

¼ cup buttermilk

2 cups (284 g) all-purpose flour

1½ cups (297 g) sugar

¾ teaspoon baking powder

¾ teaspoon baking soda

¾ teaspoon salt

½ pound (2 sticks; 227 g) unsalted butter, room temperature, cut into 1-inch pieces

Adjust an oven rack to the middle position. Preheat the oven to 350°F. Butter and flour two 8 by 2-inch round cake pans and line the bottoms with parchment paper.

In a medium bowl or liquid measuring cup, whisk the eggs, egg yolks, vanilla, sour cream, and buttermilk.

In a bowl of a stand mixer fitted with a paddle, mix the flour, sugar, baking powder, baking soda, and salt on low until combined. With the mixer running on low, add the butter one piece at a time, beating until the mixture resembles coarse sand. With the mixer still running on low, slowly add half the wet ingredients. Increase the speed to medium and beat until incorporated, about 30 seconds. With the mixer running on low, add the rest of the wet ingredients, mixing until just combined. Increase the speed to medium and beat for 20 seconds (the batter may still look a little bumpy). Scrape down the sides and bottom of the bowl, and use a spatula to mix the batter a few more times.

Divide the batter between the prepared pans and smooth the tops. Tap the pans gently on the counter 2 times each to help get rid of any bubbles. Bake 17 to 22 minutes, rotating the pans halfway through, until the cakes are golden brown and pull slightly away from the sides and a wooden skewer or toothpick inserted in the centers comes out clean.

Transfer the pans to a wire rack and let cool for 30 minutes. Turn the cakes out onto the rack, remove the parchment paper, and let cool completely. Once cool, the cakes can be wrapped in plastic and refrigerated overnight or frosted.

VARIATIONS

cardamom cake · Add 2 teaspoons ground cardamom to the dry ingredients.

spice cake (with coffee buttercream, page 141) · Add 1½ teaspoons ground cinnamon, 1 teaspoon ground cardamom, ½ teaspoon ground cloves, and ⅛ teaspoon ground black pepper to the dry ingredients.

vanilla cupcakes · Place liners in two standard 12-cup muffin tins. Fill each cup a little more than halfway full. Bake 16 to 20 minutes, until a wooden skewer or toothpick inserted into the center comes out clean. *makes 24 to 25 cupcakes*

NOTE: This recipe will work with 9 by 2-inch round cake pans and can be baked in two or three pans; for details and baking times, see page 120.

WHITE CAKE

When I'm making a cake, I usually rely on chocolate or vanilla, but every once in a while I want to make a pristine confection. White cakes are elegant looking because they are made with ingredients of the same color: shortening instead of butter, egg whites instead of yolks, and clear vanilla extract. To make the cake rich and tender, I cheat and use butter, along with the reverse creaming method (working the butter into the dry ingredients instead of creaming it with the sugars). The small amount of sour cream gives the cake a welcome bit of tang, and the end result is a snowy cake that pairs beautifully with any buttercream. *makes two 8-inch cakes*

1 cup whole milk

¼ cup sour cream

5 large egg whites

2 teaspoons pure vanilla extract (use clear vanilla for a slightly whiter cake)

2¼ cups (320 g) all-purpose flour

1½ cups (297 g) sugar

4 teaspoons baking powder

½ teaspoon salt

12 tablespoons (1½ sticks; 170 g) unsalted butter, room temperature, cut into 1-inch pieces

Adjust an oven rack to the middle position. Preheat oven to 350°F. Butter and flour two 8 by 2-inch round cake pans and line the bottoms with parchment paper.

In a medium bowl or liquid measuring cup, whisk the milk, sour cream, egg whites, and vanilla.

In a bowl of a stand mixer fitted with a paddle, mix the flour, sugar, baking powder, and salt until combined. With the mixer running on low, add the butter one piece at a time, beating until the mixture resembles coarse sand. With the mixer still running on low, slowly add half the wet ingredients. Increase the speed to medium and beat until the ingredients are incorporated, about 30 seconds. With the mixer running on low, add the rest of the wet ingredients, mixing until just combined. Increase the speed to medium and beat for 20 seconds (the batter may still look a little bumpy). Scrape down the sides and bottom of the bowl and use a spatula to mix the batter a few more times.

Divide the batter between the prepared pans and smooth the tops. Tap the pans gently on the counter 2 times each to help get rid of any bubbles. Bake 17 to 22 minutes, rotating the pans halfway through, until the cakes are golden brown and

CONTINUED

pull slightly away from the sides and a wooden skewer or toothpick inserted into the centers comes out with a faint bit of crumbs.

Transfer the pans to a wire rack and let cool 30 minutes. Turn the cakes out onto the rack, remove the parchment paper, and let cool completely. Once cool, the cakes can be wrapped in plastic and refrigerated overnight or frosted.

NOTES: This recipe will work with 9 by 2-inch round cake pans and can be baked in two or three pans; for details and baking times, see page 120.

CHOCOLATE CAKE WITH CHOCOLATE BUTTERCREAM

For many years, in late May when spring finally reached us in the North, I would drive over to take my grandma Parks out for coffee and chocolate. She loved those warm mornings together, a time to finally get out of the house after being trapped inside all winter long. She'd be waiting for me at the door, clutching her worn black purse and talking quietly to herself, her front porch smelling faintly like hair spray and drip brew. I would help her down the steps, and we would drive away, the sun beckoning to us, Louis Prima and Keely Smith swinging for us. She would tap her hands on her knees, clicking her tongue to the music. We would cruise right over to the neighborhood coffeehouse and buy iced mochas and a huge chocolate glazed doughnut for us to share. Back in the car we'd greedily sip and eat, while I drove around several of the ten thousand Minnesotan lakes, laughing at our childlike love for the bittersweet goodness coating our hands.

This cake always reminds me of her, and I feel a pang of sadness each time I make it, knowing Grandma never got a taste. We spent so many moments sharing chocolate and coffee, and it is no accident that our family cake focuses on her two favorite ingredients. She would have loved both the tender crumb and creamy chocolate buttercream. *serves 8 to 12*

1 recipe Chocolate Cake (page 129), made in two layers and cooled completely

8 ounces (226 g) bittersweet chocolate, chopped

¾ pound (3 sticks; 339 g) unsalted butter, room temperature

2 teaspoons pure vanilla extract

3 tablespoons corn syrup

¼ teaspoon salt

2 cups (226 g) confectioners' sugar

Put about 1 inch of water in a medium saucepan and bring it to a gentle boil.

Melt the chocolate in a heatproof bowl set over the pan of boiling water, being careful not to let the water touch the bottom of the bowl. Stir constantly until just melted and set aside to cool slightly.

In the bowl of a stand mixer fitted with a paddle, beat the butter on medium until light yellow and fluffy, about 3 minutes. Add the vanilla, corn syrup, and salt and beat

CONTINUED

on medium until combined. Turn the mixer to low and gradually add the confectioners' sugar. Beat at medium, stopping to scrape down the sides of the bowl as necessary, until smooth and creamy, 2 to 3 minutes. Add the chocolate and mix on low speed until no streaks remain.

TO ASSEMBLE THE CAKE: Layer and frost the cake as directed on page 120.

NOTE: This buttercream will make enough to cover the cake, but there isn't a lot left for piping or decoration. It is very rich, and I've always felt this to be the perfect amount. If you would like to decorate the cake, you can double the buttercream recipe.

VARIATION

classic birthday cake · Bake a Yellow Cake (page 132) in two or three layers and use this buttercream for the frosting. Add sprinkles on top if you like a splash of color.

CARDAMOM CAKE
WITH COFFEE BUTTERCREAM

This recipe is inspired by a spice cake with cardamom-coffee icing from Beth Dooley and Lucia Watson's book *Savoring the Seasons of the Northern Heartland*. It was the first from-scratch cake I ever made, an undertaking I decided on one Friday night while bored at work. Several hours and one gigantic mess later, I was the proud owner of a frosted spice cake. Of course, I didn't wait for the cake layers to cool completely before I applied the frosting, and I used espresso grounds in the buttercream instead of the instant coffee it called for, so it was a slightly oozy, gritty experiment. But it was delicious all the same. *serves 8 to 12*

1 recipe Cardamom Cake (page 133), made in two layers and cooled completely

1½ pounds (5 sticks; 565 g) unsalted butter, room temperature

2 teaspoons pure vanilla extract

¼ teaspoon salt

¼ cup strong coffee, cold

4 cups (452 g) confectioners' sugar

In the bowl of a stand mixer fitted with a paddle, beat the butter on medium until smooth and creamy. Scrape down the sides of the bowl and add the vanilla, salt, and coffee. Mix on low until combined; increase the speed to medium and beat 1 minute. Turn the mixer back to low and slowly add the confectioners' sugar, mixing until combined. Increase the speed to medium-high and beat until light and fluffy, stopping to scrape down the sides as necessary, 6 to 8 minutes.

TO ASSEMBLE THE CAKE: Cut each layer of the cake in half horizontally, to make a total of four layers. Put one layer, cut side up, on a serving platter, and top with ½ cup of the coffee buttercream. Use an offset spatula to spread it evenly over the layer. Repeat with two more layers and then top the cake with the remaining layer, cut side down.

Layer and frost the cake as directed on page 120.

BLACKBERRY-WHITE CHOCOLATE CAKE

I was never a fan of white chocolate until I tasted it paired with subtly tart berries. This cake is a showstopper, with a snowy white exterior swirled with jam, but luckily its beauty is not just frosting deep. Each bit of the sweet buttercream paired with the biting blackberry whispers the slightest hint of seduction. Buying good-quality white chocolate is important here, as cheaper chocolate will have a slightly artificial taste. *makes three 8-inch cakes*

1 recipe White Cake (page 135), made in three layers and cooled completely

8 ounces (226 g) good white chocolate, chopped

¾ pound (3 sticks; 339 g) unsalted butter, room temperature

1 tablespoon pure vanilla extract

3 tablespoons light corn syrup

¼ teaspoon salt

2 cups (226 g) confectioners' sugar

½ cup blackberry jam

Put about 1 inch of water in a medium saucepan and bring it to a gentle boil.

Melt the chocolate in a heatproof bowl set over the pan of boiling water, being careful not to let the water touch the bottom of the bowl. Stir constantly until just melted and set aside to cool slightly.

In the bowl of a stand mixer fitted with a paddle, beat the butter on medium until light yellow and fluffy, about 3 minutes. Add the vanilla, corn syrup, and salt and mix on medium until combined. Turn the mixer to low and gradually add the confectioners' sugar. Beat on medium until smooth and creamy, stopping to scrape down the sides of the bowl as necessary, 2 to 3 minutes. Add the white chocolate and beat on low until completely combined.

TO ASSEMBLE THE CAKE: Place one layer on a turntable or serving plate. With an offset spatula spread the top with ¾ cup buttercream. Top with 2 tablespoons of blackberry jam and spread it evenly over the surface. Place the second layer on top and frost with ¾ cup of buttercream and then 2 tablespoons of jam. Place the final layer on top and evenly coat the cake with the remaining buttercream. Use the rest of the blackberry jam to decorate if desired.

NOTE: Your favorite blackberry jam will work; Bonne Maman makes an excellent one.

Another flavor jam can be substituted for the blackberry. Something tart will work best with the sweet white chocolate.

BURNT HONEY BUTTERCREAM
CAKE WITH CHOCOLATE

Burnt honey buttercream may sound unnecessary, and perhaps a bit pretentious, but in reality it is an addictive, complex flavor, both smoky and sweet. To make it, cook honey and sugar together until dark golden brown and just smoking. Carefully pour it over beaten egg whites, then whip it with butter into buttercream perfection. A thin layer of bittersweet chocolate spread over layers of yellow cake. adds a slight crunch to each bite. *serves 8 to 12*

1 recipe Yellow Cake (page 132), made in two layers and cooled completely

8 large egg whites, room temperature

½ cup (99 g) sugar plus 1 cup (198 g) sugar

½ cup honey

¼ teaspoon salt

1½ pounds (6 sticks; 678 g) unsalted butter, room temperature, and cut into 1-inch pieces

1 teaspoon pure vanilla extract

3 ounces (85 g) bittersweet chocolate, melted

In the bowl of a stand mixer fitted with a whisk, beat the egg whites on medium until they are almost able to hold soft peaks, 5 to 7 minutes. Turn the mixer to low and add ½ cup sugar in a slow, steady stream. Beat on medium until the whites are stiff and glossy, 1 to 2 minutes. Let the whites sit in the bowl while you make the syrup.

Put the honey, 1 cup sugar, and salt in a medium saucepan. Pour ¼ cup water over the top and gently stir just enough to wet the sugar, being careful not to mix too much or get the mixture on the sides of the pan. Heat over medium heat, giving the pan a little shake every once in a while, to mix the honey and sugar as they melt. When the sugar has melted and the liquid looks clear (no sugar granules are noticeable), increase the heat to medium-high and let the liquid bubble and boil until it turns deep golden brown, 3 to 4 minutes. Remove the pan from the heat and immediately pour 2 tablespoons of water into it, carefully and gently shaking the pan to distribute it.

With the mixer on low, very carefully pour about 2 tablespoons of the hot honey caramel into the egg whites, trying not to hit the side of the bowl, and mixing until combined. (I find pouring the hot mixture into a liquid measuring cup with a pourable spout works best here.) Pour 2 more tablespoons into the egg whites and continue

CONTINUED

mixing (this will help temper the eggs so they won't cook). With the mixer on low, pour the rest of the caramel into the whites in a slow, steady stream, still trying not to hit the sides of the mixing bowl. Beat until the mixture is completely combined.

Increase the speed to medium-high and whisk until the bowl cools to room temperature. Reduce the speed to low and add the butter 1 tablespoon at a time, beating well after each addition. Increase the speed to medium and beat until the buttercream is completely smooth, 2 to 3 minutes. Add the vanilla and beat on medium for 1 to 2 minutes.

TO ASSEMBLE THE CAKE: Line two baking sheets with parchment paper. Cut each layer of the cake in half horizontally, to make a total of four layers, and place the layers on the prepared pans, cut side down. Top three of the layers with a thin coating of chocolate, spreading it thin and evenly along the whole surface of each layer. Let the chocolate set before frosting (you can put the layers in the freezer for 2 to 3 minutes to speed this up).

Put one cake layer, chocolate side up, on a turntable or serving plate and top with ¾ cup of buttercream. Repeat with two more chocolate-covered layers and then top with the remaining, chocolate-free layer. Frost the cake as directed on page 120.

NOTE: If you want an even deeper burnt flavor to your buttercream, allow the honey, salt, and sugar mixture to boil until it begins to smoke a bit; you will be able to smell it just begin to burn. Then remove the pan from the heat and continue with the directions.

LEMON MERINGUE CAKE

I've never been a fan of a traditional lemon layer cake with its mouth-puckering lemon filling and cloying seven-minute frosting; the combination somehow tastes simultaneously too tart and too sweet. But I do love cake and lemon and meringue, so I decided to come up with my own version, one with a lighter lemon flavor and a pretty toasted top. I soaked the cake layers in a lemon syrup for subtle tang, filled the middle with lemon buttercream, and then covered the cake in piles of meringue curls and swirls for an elegant dessert with delicate flavor. *makes 8 to 12 servings*

1 recipe Yellow Cake (page 132), made in two layers, still warm

⅓ cup lemon juice

⅓ cup (66 g) sugar

LEMON BUTTERCREAM FILLING

½ pound (2 sticks, 227 g) unsalted butter, room temperature

1 teaspoon grated lemon zest

2 tablespoons lemon juice

1 teaspoon vanilla extract

Pinch salt

2 cups (226 g) confectioners' sugar

MERINGUE

5 large egg whites

1 cup (198 g) sugar

¼ teaspoon salt

2 teaspoons pure vanilla extract

Mix the lemon juice and sugar in a small saucepan and boil gently over medium-high heat until a light syrup forms, 5 to 7 minutes. Brush the warm syrup over the warm cakes on a wire rack set over a baking sheet and then let them cool completely before icing.

FOR THE LEMON BUTTERCREAM FILLING: In the bowl of a stand mixer fitted with a paddle, beat the butter on medium until creamy. Add the lemon zest, lemon juice, vanilla extract, and salt, and mix on low until combined. Add the confectioners' sugar and mix on low until combined. Scrape down the sides of the mixing bowl, then increase the speed to medium and mix until light and fluffy, 3 to 5 minutes.

TO ASSEMBLE THE CAKE: Cut each cooled cake layer in half horizontally, to make a total of four layers. Put one layer cut side up on a turntable or serving plate and top with ½ cup of the lemon buttercream. Use an offset spatula or knife to smooth it out. Repeat with two more layers and then top with the final layer, cut side down. Set aside.

CONTINUED

FOR THE MERINGUE: Put about an inch of water in a medium saucepan and bring it to a gentle boil.

In the bowl of a stand mixer, stir the egg whites, sugar, and salt to combine. Put the bowl over the saucepan, being careful not to let the water touch the bottom of the bowl. Stir with a rubber spatula until the sugar is completely melted and reaches a temperature of 160°F, 4 to 5 minutes. While you are stirring, be sure to scrape down the sides of the bowl with the spatula—this will ensure no sugar grains are lurking on the sides and will help prevent the egg whites from cooking.

Remove the bowl from the heat and place it in the stand mixer fitted with a whisk. Whisk on medium-high until stiff, glossy peaks form, 8 to 10 minutes. The bowl should have cooled down to room temperature at this point. Add the vanilla and beat on low until combined.

TO FINISH THE CAKE: You won't be able to do a crumb coat with the meringue because it sets very quickly. Working fast, use a spatula to spread the meringue over the sides and top of the cake in a thick layer. I stick my offset spatula right into the meringue to get a big clump of it and then place it on the cake, gently rocking my spatula back and forth, trying not to pick up any crumbs. Once the cake is covered, you can even out the meringue and either smooth its sides and make decorative curls on the top or make curls over the entire body of the cake. Use a spoon to create curls in the meringue. Hold a kitchen blowtorch 1 to 2 inches away from the cake and touch the flame down in between the curls. The curls will toast and brown (if the curls set on fire, you can blow them out). Do this until you are happy with the color of the cake.

If you do not have a torch, you can brown the meringue under a broiler, using a heatproof plate to hold the cake (a cake stand will not work here). Adjust your oven rack so the cake will be a few inches below the broiler. Preheat the broiler. Place the cake under the broiler for 45 to 60 seconds, until the tips of the meringue curls turn brown. Keep a close eye on the cake! The meringue can burn easily.

NOTE: For a cake with a very light lemon flavor, skip brushing the cake layers with the lemon syrup.

MINT CHOCOLATE CAKE

When I was nine years old my baby brother was born, two weeks late, on my birthday. At the time I wasn't very happy about the arrangement, as I had to begrudgingly share my one special day with an adorable baby. Over the years my feelings changed for the better, and we eventually became friends. However, it was only recently that we came to an agreement on what kind of cake should be served at our yearly birthday party. Mint and chocolate have always been at the top of our list of favorites, so this cake should have been an obvious choice years ago. Swiss Meringue Buttercream spiked with crème de menthe makes this rich and indulgent, with a mint flavor that is not too strong and complements the chocolate exactly right. *makes two 8-inch cakes*

1 recipe Chocolate Cake (page 129), made in two layers and cooled completely

8 large egg whites

2¼ cups (446 g) sugar

¼ teaspoon salt

1½ pounds (6 sticks; 678 g) unsalted butter, room temperature

2 tablespoons crème de menthe

½ teaspoon mint extract plus more to taste

1 teaspoon pure vanilla extract

½ cup (85 g) chocolate chips, chopped small (optional; see note)

Put about 1 inch of water in a medium saucepan and bring it to a gentle boil.

In the bowl of a stand mixer, stir the egg whites, sugar, and salt until combined. Put the bowl over the saucepan, being careful not to let the water touch the bottom of the bowl. Stir with a rubber spatula until the sugar is completely melted, and the mixture reaches a temperature of 160°F, about 4 to 5 minutes. While you are stirring, be sure to scrape down the sides of the bowl with the spatula—this will ensure no sugar grains are lurking on the sides and will help prevent the egg whites from cooking.

Remove the bowl from the heat and place it in the stand mixer fitted with a whisk. Whisk the mixture on medium-high until stiff, glossy peaks form, 8 to 10 minutes. With the mixer running on low, add the butter, 1 to 2 tablespoons at a time, beating well after each addition until incorporated. Add the crème de menthe, mint extract, and vanilla. Beat again and then taste test. If you want your buttercream to have a stronger mint flavor, add more mint extract ½ teaspoon at a time, until you are happy with the taste. Add the chocolate (if using) and stir with a spatula to combine. Layer and frost the cake directed on pages 121 to 122.

RASPBERRY CREAM CAKE

Strawberry shortcake is a summertime favorite, but I often find it lacking, with shortbread that ends up soggy and berries that are either out of season or a soupy mess. Inspired by America's Test Kitchen, I decided to revamp the whole business in party cake form. I used my yellow cake as a base, swapped raspberries for the strawberries, and topped things off with a cream cheese whipped frosting studded with vanilla beans. The result? Amazing. *makes two 8-inch cakes*

1 recipe Yellow Cake (page 132), made in two layers and cooled completely

6 ounces (170 g) cream cheese, room temperature

½ cup (99 g) sugar

½ teaspoon pure vanilla extract

1 vanilla bean, seeds scraped

¼ teaspoon salt

2 to 3 drops pink food coloring (optional)

1½ cups heavy cream

12 ounces (340 g) raspberries, plus more for decorating the top

Fresh flowers, for decorating (optional)

In the bowl of a stand mixer fitted with a paddle, beat the cream cheese on medium until smooth. Add the sugar, vanilla extract, vanilla bean seeds, salt, and food coloring (if using) and beat on medium until smooth and light, about 3 minutes. Scrape down the sides of the bowl and fit the mixer with the whisk. With the mixer running on low, slowly add the heavy cream, whisking until fully combined. Increase the speed to medium-high and beat until stiff peaks form, stopping to scrape down the sides of the bowl as necessary, 2 to 3 minutes.

TO ASSEMBLE THE CAKE: Put one layer on a turntable or serving platter and top with 1 cup of the whipped cream. Arrange the raspberries evenly over the whipped cream. Top with the second layer and then coat the cake with the remaining whipped cream. The cake can be served immediately, or chilled for up to 2 hours before serving. Decorate with more raspberries, or fresh flowers, if desired.

VARIATION

raspberry-rose cream cake · Add 1 tablespoon rose water to the whipped cream, along with the vanilla extract.

NOTE: If your berries are out of season, you may want to sprinkle them with 1 or 2 tablespoons of sugar just before assembling. The sugar will cause the raspberries to leak a little bit of juice as the cake sits.

For even more berry flavor, spread ½ cup (170 g) of raspberry jam on the bottom layer before arranging the raspberries on top.

VEGAN CHOCOLATE CAKE

It's always been important to me to have a dessert option available for everyone when they stop by my house. These days, more and more of my friends have food allergies or choose not to eat dairy, so I decided to come up with some treats for them. This cake is inspired by the Chocolate Cake with Chocolate Buttercream (page 137) as well as one particularly popular vegan cake recipe that everyone seems to use from the *Moosewood Collective* cookbook. It's full of chocolate flavor and is wonderfully moist; your non-vegan guests won't even know it's dairy-free. *makes 8 to 12 servings*

1 cup unsweetened soy milk, coconut milk, or almond milk

1 cup coffee, room temperature (water will work, too)

½ cup canola oil

2 teaspoons pure vanilla extract

2 tablespoons apple cider vinegar

2 cups (284 g) all-purpose flour

2 cups (396 g) sugar

¾ cup (75 g) Dutch process cocoa powder

1 teaspoon baking soda

½ teaspoon baking powder

1 teaspoon salt

Adjust an oven rack to the middle position. Preheat the oven to 350°F. Butter and flour two 8 by 2-inch round cake pans and line the bottom with parchment paper.

In a medium bowl or liquid measuring cup, whisk the soy milk, coffee, canola oil, vanilla, and apple cider vinegar.

In the bowl of a stand mixer fitted with a paddle, mix the flour, sugar, cocoa powder, baking soda, baking powder, and salt on low until combined. (If the cocoa powder is lumpy, you can sift it into the other ingredients.) With the mixer running on low, slowly add the soy milk mixture, mixing until combined. Using a spatula, give the batter a couple of turns to make sure it is fully mixed. Pour the batter evenly into the prepared pans. Bake 25 to 35 minutes, until a wooden skewer or toothpick inserted into the cake comes out with the tiniest bit of crumb.

Transfer the pans to a wire rack and let cool 30 minutes. Turn the cakes out onto the rack, remove the parchment paper and let cool completely. Once cool, the cakes can be wrapped in plastic and refrigerated overnight or frosted.

CONTINUED

DAIRY-FREE CHOCOLATE FROSTING

Vegan chocolate in bar form can be rather expensive, and often hard to track down. I found some semisweet chocolate chip brands didn't contain dairy and worked well in this recipe.

This frosting will make just enough to cover the cake, so there isn't a lot left for piping or decoration. It is very rich and the perfect amount. If you would like to decorate the cake, you can double the recipe. *makes about 4 cups*

1⅓ cups (226 g) vegan semisweet chocolate chips (make sure the brand you use doesn't contain dairy)

¾ cup (138 g) vegetable shortening

2 teaspoons pure vanilla extract

3 tablespoons corn syrup

¼ teaspoon salt

2 cups (226 g) confectioners' sugar

Put about 1 inch of water in a medium saucepan and bring it to a gentle boil.

Melt the chocolate in a heatproof bowl set over the pan of water, being careful not to let the water touch the bottom of the bowl. Stir constantly until just melted and set aside to cool slightly.

In the bowl of a stand mixer fitted with a paddle, beat the shortening on medium for 1 minute, getting out any lumps. Add the vanilla, corn syrup, and salt and beat on medium until combined. Turn the mixer to low and gradually add the confectioners' sugar. Then beat on medium until smooth and creamy, stopping to scrape down the bowl as necessary, 2 to 3 minutes. Add the chocolate and mix on low until blended. Use immediately.

TO ASSEMBLE THE CAKE: Follow the directions for layering and frosting cakes on page 120.

TRIPLE CHOCOLATE CUPCAKES

The base of these little beauties is a simple chocolate cake filled with even more chocolate, in rich ganache form. They are then topped with a creamy white chocolate buttercream, and each bite is pure bliss. Chocolate + chocolate + chocolate. I can't think of a better equation. *makes 16 to 17 cupcakes*

GANACHE FILLING

4 ounces (113 g) bittersweet chocolate, chopped into small pieces

⅓ cup heavy cream

CUPCAKES

3 ounces (85 g) bittersweet chocolate

½ cup freshly brewed coffee, hot

¼ cup buttermilk

¼ cup canola oil

2 large eggs

1 teaspoon pure vanilla extract

1 cup (142 g) all-purpose flour

1 cup (198 g) sugar

¼ cup (25 g) Dutch process cocoa powder

1 teaspoon baking soda

½ teaspoon salt

WHITE CHOCOLATE BUTTERCREAM

8 ounces (226 g) good white chocolate, chopped

¾ pound (3 sticks; 339 g) unsalted butter, room temperature

1 tablespoon pure vanilla extract

3 tablespoons light corn syrup

¼ teaspoon salt

2 cups (226 g) confectioners' sugar

FOR THE GANACHE FILLING: Place the chocolate in a medium bowl. Heat the cream in a small saucepan until it is simmering and just about to boil. Pour the cream over the chocolate, then cover the bowl with plastic wrap and let it sit for 5 minutes.

Remove the plastic wrap and whisk until the chocolate mixture is completely smooth. Place the bowl in the refrigerator until the mixture is just chilled, about 20 minutes. Do not let it completely harden in the fridge.

FOR THE CUPCAKES: Adjust an oven rack to the middle position. Preheat the oven to 350°F. Place liners in two standard 12-cup muffin tins, filling 17 of the cups.

Put the chocolate in a small bowl. Pour the coffee over it and cover with a piece of plastic wrap. In a medium bowl or liquid measuring cup, whisk the buttermilk, canola oil, eggs, and vanilla.

CONTINUED

In the bowl of a stand mixer fitted with a paddle, mix the flour, sugar, cocoa powder, baking soda, and salt on low until combined. (If the cocoa powder is lumpy, you can sift it into the other ingredients.) With the mixer running on low, slowly add the buttermilk mixture. Increase the speed to medium and mix until combined, 20 to 30 seconds.

Whisk the chocolate and coffee until combined. With the mixer running on low, slowly pour the coffee mixture into the batter and mix until just combined. Using a spatula, give the batter a couple of turns to make sure it is fully mixed.

Scoop ¼ cup of batter into each cup of the prepared muffin tins. Remove the ganache from the fridge and place 1 rounded teaspoon in each muffin cup on top of the batter, directly in the center.

Bake 14 to 17 minutes, until the cupcakes are set and firm to the touch.

Transfer the tin to a wire rack and let cool about 15 minutes. Remove the cupcakes from the tin and let cool completely before frosting each with a heaping layer of White Chocolate Buttercream.

FOR THE BUTTERCREAM: Put about 1 inch of water in a medium saucepan and bring it to a gentle boil.

Melt the chocolate in a heatproof bowl set over the pan of boiling water, being careful not to let the water touch the bottom of the bowl. Stir constantly until just melted and set aside to cool slightly.

In the bowl of a stand mixer fitted with a paddle, beat the butter on medium until light yellow and fluffy, about 3 minutes. Add the vanilla, corn syrup, and salt and mix on medium until combined. Turn the mixer to low and gradually add the confectioners' sugar. Beat on medium until smooth and creamy, stopping to scrape down the sides of the bowl as necessary, 2 to 3 minutes. Add the white chocolate and beat on low until completely combined.

NOTE: Be sure not to fill the muffin cups too full or the batter will spill over the sides during baking.

VANILLA CUPCAKES
WITH BROWN BUTTER BUTTERCREAM

Browning butter isn't difficult to do, and the results are magical. Cooking the butter down to golden goodness gives it a nutty, toasty flavor that mixes well with both sweet and savory dishes. I like to use brown butter in many things, but my favorite way is to whip it up into a buttercream. The vanilla base of these cupcakes complements the sweetened brown butter just right, and the results are heavenly. *makes 24 to 25 cupcakes, and 4 cups of buttercream*

1 recipe Yellow Cake (page 132), baked into cupcakes, or in two layers and cooled completely

½ pound (2 sticks; 227 g) unsalted butter for browning

½ pound (2 sticks; 227 g) unsalted butter, room temperature

2 ounces (57 g) cream cheese, room temperature

¼ cup heavy cream

2 teaspoons pure vanilla extract

½ teaspoon salt

4 cups (452 g) confectioners' sugar

Brown ½ pound of butter as directed on page 313. Pour the brown butter into a heatproof, freezer-safe bowl and let cool for 10 minutes. Then place the bowl in the freezer and let chill until solid, about 30 minutes (you can also put it in the fridge to cool, but it will take a bit longer). When the butter is solid (but not frozen!), transfer it to the bowl of a stand mixer fitted with a paddle.

Add the remaining ½ pound of butter to the brown butter and beat on medium until smooth. Add the cream cheese and beat on medium until smooth and creamy. Add the heavy cream, vanilla, and salt and mix on low to combine. With the mixer running on low, slowly add the confectioners' sugar and beat until combined. Increase the speed to medium-high and beat until light and fluffy, stopping to scrape down the sides of the bowl as necessary, 6 to 8 minutes. Using an offset spatula, spread the top of each cupcake with a heaping layer of buttercream.

VANILLA CUPCAKES
WITH BERRY SWIRL BUTTERCREAM

This Berry Swirl Buttercream is a simple way to add some elegance to your cupcakes or cake. Adding a couple tablespoons of jam along the seams of a pastry bag adds beautiful swirls that look like more work than they actually are. I've paired this buttercream with vanilla cupcakes, but it also tastes delicious with Chocolate Ganache Cupcakes (page 165). ***makes 24 to 25 cupcakes***

1 Yellow Cake (page 132), baked into cupcakes and cooled completely

2 to 4 tablespoons blueberry or raspberry jam

Swiss Meringue Buttercream (page 125) or American Buttercream (page 125)

Cut the tip of a pastry bag and place a closed star piping tip (Ateco #848) inside the bag. Place 1 tablespoon of the jam on the inside side seam of the bag and, using a spoon, smear it up and down the seam in a wide strip. Repeat along the other seam, using 1 tablespoon of jam. Carefully add buttercream to the bag, trying not to disturb the jam and leaving a little space at the top so the buttercream doesn't fill the entire bag.

Working with one cupcake at a time, start with the pastry tip on the outside edge of the cupcake and work your way around the edge of the cupcake. Spiral around, working toward the center. The jam inside the bag will make pretty lines and swirls in the buttercream as you spiral around. If you need to refill your bag, place more jam on the seams each time.

CHOCOLATE GANACHE CUPCAKES
WITH BASIL BUTTERCREAM

I had my first taste of basil and chocolate almost two decades ago, out with friends at Lucia's restaurant in Minneapolis. Our server recommended the chocolate cake paired with the basil ice cream, and the combination sounded so intriguing we decided to trust him. The bright blue of my shirt, the buzz of voices at tables surrounding us, the candles speckling the dimly lit room, and chocolate and basil devoured alternately bite by bite is forever etched in my mind. Over the years I've re-created those flavors in many applications, but this cupcake and buttercream pairing is by far my favorite. The basil flavor grows with intensity over time, and the creamy ganache centers are downright indulgent. *makes 16 to 17 cupcakes, and about 4 cups of buttercream*

GANACHE FILLING

4 ounces (113 g) bittersweet
   chocolate, chopped

⅓ cup heavy cream

GANACHE CUPCAKES

3 ounces (85 g) bittersweet chocolate

½ cup freshly brewed coffee, hot

¼ cup buttermilk

¼ cup canola oil

2 large eggs

1 teaspoon pure vanilla extract

1 cup (142 g) all-purpose flour

1 cup (198 g) sugar

¼ cup (25 g) Dutch process cocoa
   powder

1 teaspoon baking soda

½ teaspoon salt

BASIL BUTTERCREAM

1½ cups whole milk

½ cup heavy cream

1 cup packed basil leaves

1¾ cups (347 g) sugar

½ cup (71 g) all-purpose flour

½ teaspoon salt

¾ pound (3 sticks; 339 g) unsalted
   butter, room temperature, cut
   into small pieces

2 teaspoons pure vanilla extract

3 to 4 drops green food coloring
   (optional)

CONTINUED

FOR THE GANACHE FILLING: Place the chocolate in a medium bowl. Heat the cream in a small saucepan, until it is simmering and just about to boil. Pour the cream over the chocolate, then cover the bowl with plastic wrap and let it sit for 5 minutes.

Remove the plastic wrap and whisk until the chocolate mixture is completely smooth. Place the bowl in the refrigerator until it is just chilled, about 20 minutes. Do not let it completely harden in the fridge.

FOR THE CUPCAKES: Adjust an oven rack to the middle position. Preheat the oven to 350°F. Place liners in two standard 12-cup muffin tins, filling 17 of the cups.

Put the bittersweet chocolate in a small bowl. Pour the coffee over it and cover with a piece of plastic wrap. In a medium bowl or liquid measuring cup, whisk the buttermilk, canola oil, eggs, and vanilla.

In the bowl of a stand mixer fitted with a paddle, mix the flour, sugar, cocoa powder, baking soda, and salt on low until combined. (If the cocoa powder is lumpy, you can sift it into the other ingredients.) With the mixer running on low, slowly add the buttermilk mixture. Increase the speed to medium and beat until combined, 20 to 30 seconds.

Whisk the chocolate and coffee until combined. With the mixer running on low, slowly pour the coffee mixture into the batter and mix until just combined. Using a spatula, give the batter a couple of turns to make sure it is fully mixed.

Scoop ¼ cup of batter into each cup of the prepared muffin tins. Remove the ganache from the fridge and place 1 rounded teaspoon in each muffin cup, on top of the batter, directly in the center.

Bake 14 to 17 minutes, until the cupcakes are set and firm to the touch.

Transfer the tin to a wire rack and let cool for about 15 minutes. Remove the cupcakes from the pan and let cool completely on a wire rack before frosting. When cool, use an offset spatula to spread the top of each cupcake with a heaping layer of buttercream.

NOTE: Be sure not to fill the muffin cups too full or the batter will spill over the sides during baking.

FOR THE BASIL BUTTERCREAM: Combine the milk, heavy cream, and basil in a medium saucepan. Heat gently over medium heat, until just simmering; remove from the heat. Let cool and refrigerate for at least 2 hours and up to overnight. Remove the basil leaves from the cream, squeezing any "juice" from the leaves into the cream.

In a medium heavy-bottomed saucepan, whisk the sugar, flour, and salt. Add the cream mixture and stir together until combined. Cook over medium heat, stirring constantly with a spatula, until the mixture comes to a gentle boil. Reduce the heat slightly, switch to a whisk, and whisk constantly until the mixture has thickened and resembles potato soup, 10 to 15 minutes. The mixture can easily burn on the bottom, so keep a close eye on it while it cooks.

Transfer the mixture to the bowl of a stand mixer fitted with a whisk. Beat on high until the bowl cools down to room temperature, 7 to 9 minutes (alternately, you can skip beating and put the bowl in the refrigerator instead to cool the milk mixture to room temperature, 30 to 40 minutes. Then continue with directions and add butter to the mixture). Reduce the speed to low and add the butter, mixing until thoroughly incorporated. Increase the speed to medium-high and beat until the frosting is light and fluffy, 4 to 5 minutes. Add the vanilla and food coloring (if using) and continue mixing on low until combined. If the frosting is too soft, put the bowl in the refrigerator to chill slightly, about 10 minutes, and then beat again until it is light and creamy.

VARIATION

lavender buttercream · Omit the basil and green food coloring. Add 1 tablespoon dried culinary lavender to the milk and heavy cream and continue with the recipe as directed. Add a few drops of purple food coloring if desired.

CLASSIC CHEESECAKE

In all honesty, before writing this book I hadn't made many noteworthy cheesecakes. They were delicious, but they often cracked at the top and were not always perfectly smooth. After spending weeks making one cheesecake after the other, I discovered some helpful tricks. Scraping down the bowl obsessively and beating the cream cheese for an extended period of time made for a creamy, smooth filling. Banging the pan against the counter to bring any air bubbles to the surface resulted in a cheesecake that rose perfectly flat and did not crack. Double wrapping the cheesecake pan in foil (a helpful tip from Tara O'Brady) ensured white sides that didn't overbake. My cheesecakes are now dreamy, with a creamy base and a crisp graham cracker crust. *makes one 9-inch cheesecake*

CRUST

2 cups (200 g) graham cracker crumbs (or 14 whole graham crackers, pulsed in a food processor)

¼ cup (50 g) sugar

5 tablespoons (72 g) unsalted butter, melted

CHEESECAKE

2 pounds (904 g) cream cheese, room temperature

1 cup (198 g) sugar

2 cups sour cream

1 tablespoon pure vanilla extract

½ teaspoon salt

2 tablespoons (29 g) unsalted butter, melted and cooled to room temperature

3 large eggs, room temperature

1 large yolk, room temperature

1 recipe Sour Cherry Sauce (page 314) or Chocolate Ganache (page 309) (optional)

FOR THE CRUST: Adjust an oven rack to the middle position. Preheat the oven to 325°F.

Whisk the graham cracker crumbs and sugar in a medium bowl. Add the melted butter and mix with a spatula until evenly incorporated. Press the mixture onto the bottom of a 9-inch springform pan and bake 10 minutes. Remove from the oven and let cool. After the pan has cooled, wrap just the sides in two layers of aluminum foil, with the shiny side facing out (this helps keep the sides of the cheesecake from browning).

FOR THE CHEESECAKE: In the bowl of a stand mixer fitted with a paddle, beat the cream cheese on medium until light, fluffy, and completely smooth,

CONTINUED

4 to 5 minutes. Scrape down the bowl repeatedly, making sure that by the end every tiny speck of cream cheese is silky smooth. Add the sugar and beat on medium until completely incorporated, stopping to scrape down the sides of the bowl, 2 to 3 minutes. Add the sour cream, vanilla, and salt and beat on medium for 2 to 3 minutes. Add the butter and mix on low until combined. With the mixer running on medium, add the eggs and the egg yolk one at a time, beating after each addition just until combined and stopping to scrape down the sides of the bowl as needed. Using a spatula, give the filling a couple of turns to make sure it is fully mixed.

Pour the filling over the cooled crust and use an offset spatula to smooth the top. Bang the bottom of the springform pan on the counter to help get rid of any air bubbles (I do this quite a few times, until most of the air bubbles that appear on the surface pop).

Set a roasting pan on the floor of the oven and fill it with 4 quarts of warm water. Place the springform pan on the oven rack and bake 1 hour without opening the door. Check the cheesecake after 1 hour. The outer ring (2 to 3 inches) of the cheesecake should be slightly puffed and fairly firm, and the center should be set but still a bit jiggly when wiggled gently, resembling Jell-O. If the outer ring is not firm, let the cheesecake bake another 10 to 15 minutes. If it is done, turn off the heat, open the oven door just a crack, and let the cheesecake rest and cool in the warm, humid oven for 30 minutes.

Transfer the pan to a wire rack and let cool 5 to 10 minutes. Remove the foil from the pan, and carefully run a thin knife or offset spatula around the cake to help loosen it from the pan (this will help prevent cracking as it cools). Once the cake is completely cool, place a piece of parchment paper over the top of the pan (to keep condensation off the top of the cheesecake) and transfer to the refrigerator. Let chill at least 6 hours or overnight.

To remove the cheesecake from the pan, run a thin, offset spatula between the sides of the cake and the pan and then gently remove the sides. Slide the spatula between the bottom of the crust and the pan to loosen and then carefully slide the cheesecake onto a serving plate. Let the cheesecake come to room temperature before serving.

Serve the cheesecake plain, with Sour Cherry Sauce on the side, or use an offset spatula to spread Chocolate Ganache evenly over the top. Let the ganache set before slicing.

NOTES: There is much debate on the best way to bake a cheesecake. I've always used a roasting pan of water on the floor of the oven instead of immersing the cheesecake in a water bath. The steam from the water helps prevent the cheesecake from drying and cracking. Many people argue that a water bath helps create a creamier cheesecake, but I haven't noticed a significant difference, so I've stuck to my tried-and-true technique.

CHOCOLATE CHEESECAKE

We made a version of this cake at the Blue Heron, and it was much sought after. In fact, there was a group of college students from China who came in daily just for this dessert. One woman in particular would order two pieces of cake cut into one big triangle and a giant iced mocha to wash it all down. She told me she had never had cheesecake before she moved to America, and her eyes would light up every time she ordered her daily double slice. I was always rather awestruck at her afternoon indulgence and could never decide if eating cheesecake every single day was the best idea or the worst. I am pretty sure it was the best. *makes 8 to 12 servings*

CRUST

20 Oreo cookies

5 tablespoons (72 g) unsalted butter, melted

CHEESECAKE

2 pounds (904 g) cream cheese, room temperature

1¼ cups (248 g) sugar

1 cup (227 g) sour cream, room temperature

2 teaspoons pure vanilla extract

½ teaspoon salt

2 tablespoons (29 g) unsalted butter, melted and cooled to room temperature

3 large eggs, room temperature

1 large yolk, room temperature

8 ounces (226 g) bittersweet chocolate, melted and cooled to room temperature

Chocolate Ganache (page 309)

FOR THE CRUST: Adjust an oven rack to the middle position. Preheat the oven to 325°F.

Pulse the Oreos in a food processor fitted with the steel blade until they are broken down into crumbs. You should have 2½ cups (240 g) of crumbs. Add the butter and pulse 5 to 7 times, until incorporated. Press the mixture into the bottom of a 9-inch springform pan and bake for 10 minutes. Remove from the oven and let cool. After the pan has cooled, wrap just the sides in two layers of aluminum foil, with the shiny side facing out (this helps keep the sides of the cheesecake from browning).

FOR THE CHEESECAKE: In the bowl of a stand mixer fitted with a paddle, beat the cream cheese on medium until light, fluffy, and completely smooth, 5 to 7 minutes. Scrape down the bowl repeatedly, making sure that by the end every tiny speck of cream cheese is silky smooth. Add the sugar and beat on medium until completely

CONTINUED

incorporated, stopping to scrape down the sides of the bowl, 3 minutes. Add the sour cream, vanilla, and salt and beat on medium for 2 to 3 minutes. Add the butter and mix on low until combined. With the mixer running on medium, add the eggs and the egg yolk one at a time, beating after each addition, just until combined and stopping to scrape down the sides of the bowl as needed. Add the melted chocolate and mix on low until combined. Use a spatula to mix the filling until it is a uniform color (this may take a few minutes). Check the bottom of the bowl for any white streaks.

Pour the filling over the cooled crust—it will come right up to the top—and use an offset spatula to smooth the top. Bang the bottom of the springform pan on the counter to help get rid of any air bubbles (I do this quite a few times, until most of the air bubbles that appear on the surface pop).

Set a roasting pan on the floor of the oven and fill it with 4 quarts of warm water. Place the springform pan on the middle oven rack and bake for 1 hour without opening the door. Check the cheesecake after 1 hour. The outer ring (2 to 3 inches) of the cheesecake should be slightly puffed and fairly firm, and the center should be set but still a bit jiggly when wiggled gently, resembling Jell-O. If the outer ring is not puffed, let the cheesecake cook another 10 to 15 minutes. If it is done, turn off the heat, open the oven door just a crack, and let the cheesecake rest and cool in the warm, humid oven for 30 minutes.

Transfer the pan to a wire rack and let cool 5 to 10 minutes. Remove the foil from the pan, and carefully run a thin knife or offset spatula around the cake to help loosen it from the pan (this will help prevent cracking as it cools). Once the cake is completely cool, place a piece of parchment paper over the top of the pan (to keep condensation off the top of the cheesecake) and transfer to the refrigerator. Let chill at least 6 hours or overnight.

To remove the cheesecake from the pan, run a thin offset spatula between the sides of the cake and then gently remove the sides. Slide the spatula between the bottom of the crust and the pan to loosen and then carefully slide the cheesecake onto a serving plate. Pour the chocolate ganache onto the top of the cheesecake, right in the center. Using an offset spatula, cover the whole top with the ganache, carefully smoothing it out as you move it to the edges. If you want chocolate drips down the side of the cheesecake, gently push a little bit of the ganache over the edge until it starts to cascade down. Let the ganache set before slicing and let the cheesecake come to room temperature before serving.

(ALMOST) NO-BAKE CHEESECAKE
WITH JAM SWIRL

I've found this cheesecake to be a great substitute for the real deal. It is creamy and delicious, perfect for hot summer days. You need to bake it only a few minutes to ensure a crisp crust and the smooth filling easily sets in the refrigerator. The berry swirls add a bit of fruity tartness to the cheesecake that I find delicious, but you could leave it out and top it instead with Chocolate Ganache (page 309). *makes one 9-inch cheesecake*

CRUST

2 cups (200 g) graham cracker crumbs

¼ cup (50 g) sugar

5 tablespoons (72 g) unsalted butter, melted

CHEESECAKE

2 pounds (904 g) cream cheese, room temperature

¾ cup (149 g) sugar

1 teaspoon pure vanilla extract

½ teaspoon salt

1¼ cups heavy cream

½ cup jam of your choice

FOR THE CRUST: Adjust an oven rack to the middle position. Preheat the oven to 325°F.

Put the graham cracker crumbs and sugar in a medium bowl and whisk. Pour the melted butter over the top and stir with a spatula until combined. Press the mixture into a 9-inch springform pan and bake 10 to 12 minutes, or until the crust is golden. Remove from the oven and set aside to cool.

FOR THE CHEESECAKE: In a stand mixer fitted with a paddle, beat the cream cheese on high until smooth and creamy, about 3 minutes. Add the sugar, vanilla, and salt and beat on medium until light and smooth, about 3 minutes. Transfer the cream cheese mixture to a large bowl and set aside. Clean the mixing bowl if you have only one.

In a stand mixer fitted with a whisk, beat the cream (in the clean bowl) on low for 30 to 45 seconds. Increase the speed to medium and continue beating 30 to 45 seconds. Increase the speed to high and continue beating until stiff peaks form, 30 to 60 seconds.

CONTINUED

With a rubber spatula, stir about one-third of the whipped cream into the cream cheese mixture and fold until completely combined. Add the remaining whipped cream and fold until combined and no streaks remain.

Scrape the filling over the cooled crust and smooth the top with an offset spatula. Decorate the top with jam swirls (see below). Refrigerate the cheesecake until firm, about 4 hours or up to 1 day.

FOR THE JAM SWIRLS: Combine the jam and 1 tablespoon water in a small saucepan. Warm over low heat until the jam is loose. Let the mixture cool a bit. Drop the jam in circles over the top of the cheesecake and use a skewer or knife to drag it through the top of the cheesecake, making swirls.

chapter four

PIES + TARTS

When I started learning to make pie, I checked out many pie books from the library, looking for advice on how to make the perfect one. Each introduction reassured me not to worry; it was all quite simple. One month later, after making piles of pies with soggy bottom crusts and sickly sweet, leaky fillings, or others with rock-hard tops and mouth-puckering fruit, I was not buying into this easy-as-pie business.

So the experimenting began. I worked on the base first and eventually decided on an all-butter crust. I added a little sugar to the dough, as well as an egg yolk and a tablespoon of sour cream, which resulted in a tender, slightly sweet dough. Developing consistent, flaky layers was a must, and just a bit of folding at the end helped ensure them without overworking the dough. A preheated baking sheet and a glass pie plate were essential tools in getting a bottom crust that was golden brown and perfectly cooked.

Filling was the next battle. I started with the thickener, wanting flour to be my go-to so I could use an ingredient I always had on hand, but found that it often muddled the flavor. Tapioca worked great, but made the filling too jelly-like for my tastes. Cornstarch ended up being my winner; it kept the flavor pure and thickened without being gummy. I also remembered a trick from *Cooks Illustrated*: adding a peeled, grated apple along with everything else. Some apples contain a good amount of pectin, and this thickening power meant I didn't have to add quite as much cornstarch, and the sweetness of the apple balanced any tart flavors in the filling without having to add extra sugar.

Next I moved on to the fruit itself. I thought back to a book I had read early on in my quest, *The Pie and Pastry Bible* by Rose Levy Beranbaum. Ms. Beranbaum makes her pie fillings by tossing peeled and sliced fruit with sugar and salt and letting it sit until the fruit releases its juice. After straining the fruit, she boils down the juice to make a thin syrup, which is then cooled, mixed with the reserved fruit, and used to fill the pie. Lo and behold, this method gave me the best pies yet. After further testing, I found I liked to add a little more sugar to the juice before boiling it down. I also took some advice from Tara O'Brady's cookbook, *Seven Spoons*, and added butter, vanilla extract, and some heavy cream or liqueur (depending on the recipe) to the juices as they cooled.

There was one more piece to fine-tune: the exact amount of fruit to add. Most recipes call for how much whole fruit to start with, but I found I didn't always peel, core, and slice apples, pears, and peaches consistently. Sometimes in a rush I didn't cut close enough to the core, and had less fruit to work with. Other times I measured incorrectly, or accidentally bought medium-size fruit instead of large. I decided that knowing how much fruit was needed after it was peeled and sliced would help keep things more consistent. Now, after baking many pies with my tried-and-true method, I have dependable results and beautiful, delicious pies each and every time.

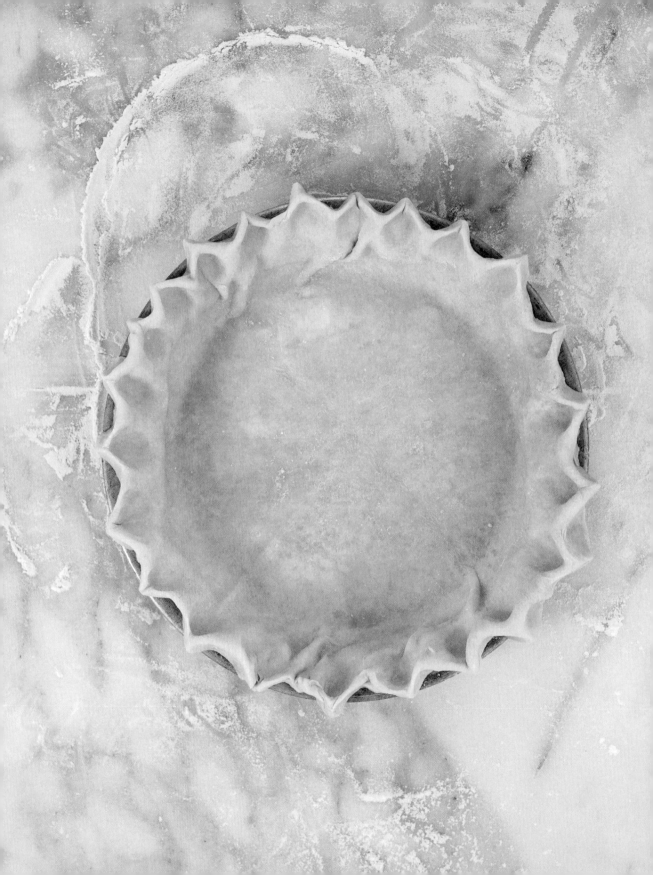

SINGLE-CRUST PIE DOUGH

Single-crust pie dough is usually partially baked or fully baked before the filling goes inside it. When a pie filling doesn't need a very long baking time, the pie crust needs to be baked a bit first so it doesn't turn out soggy and undercooked; for example, see Chocolate Meringue Pie (page 211). Of course, when using a no-bake filling, the crust needs to be fully baked for assembling the pie. *makes enough for 1 single-crust 9-inch pie*

9 tablespoons (128 g) unsalted butter, cut into 8 to 10 pieces

1 large egg yolk (optional)

1¼ cups (179 g) all-purpose flour

1 tablespoon sugar

½ teaspoon salt

Put the butter in a bowl and place in the freezer. Fill a medium liquid measuring cup with water and add plenty of ice. Let both the butter and the ice water sit for 5 to 10 minutes.

Put the egg yolk in a small liquid measuring cup. Pour in 2 tablespoons of the very cold water and stir to combine. (If not using the egg yolk, just add the cold water to the dry ingredients.)

In the bowl of a stand mixer fitted with a paddle, combine the flour, sugar, and salt on low. Add half the chilled butter and mix on low until it just starts to break down, about 1 minute. Add the rest of the butter and continue mixing on low until the butter is broken down and in various sizes (some butter will be incorporated into the dough, some will still be a bit large, but most should be about the size of small peas). Stop the mixer and use your hands to check for any large pieces of butter that didn't get mixed or any dry patches of dough on the bottom of the bowl; break up the butter and incorporate the dry flour as best you can. With the mixer running on low, slowly add the egg yolk mixture and mix until the dough starts to come together but still is quite shaggy (if the dough is not coming together, add more water 1 tablespoon at a time until it does).

Dump the dough out on a lightly floured work surface and flatten it slightly into a square. Gather any loose/dry pieces that won't stick to the dough and place them on top of the square. Gently fold the dough over onto itself and flatten again. Repeat this process 3 or 4 more times, until all the loose pieces are worked into the dough. Be

CONTINUED

very gentle with your movements, being careful not to overwork the dough. Flatten the dough one last time into a 6-inch disc and wrap in plastic wrap. Refrigerate for 30 minutes (and up to 2 days) before using.

When ready to use, lightly flour a work surface and roll the dough to a 12-inch circle. Gently fold the dough in quarters and place it in the pie plate. Unfold the dough, letting the excess dough drape over the edges. Gently press the dough into the bottom and trim the overhang to 1 inch past the lip. Tuck the overhang, so the folded edge lies on the edge of the pan. Crimp the edge of the dough, using your fingers (see facing page). Place the pie plate in the freezer and freeze until firm, 20 to 30 minutes.

Adjust an oven rack to the lowest position. Preheat the oven to 425°F. Place a baking sheet on the oven rack (the preheated baking sheet helps crisp the bottom of the pie crust). Remove the pie plate from the freezer and line the pie shell with parchment paper, covering the edges to prevent burning. Fill the center with pie weights and bake as directed.

NOTE

partially baked crust · Bake 25 to 28 minutes, until the dough is golden brown and no longer wet. Transfer the pie plate to a wire rack. Carefully remove the pie weights and parchment paper. Finish the pie as directed in the recipe.

for a fully baked crust · Bake 25 to 28 minutes, until the dough is golden brown and no longer wet. Remove the pie plate from the oven and carefully remove the pie weights and parchment paper. Return the pie plate to the oven and continue to bake 8 to 12 minutes, until deep golden brown. Transfer the pie plate to a wire rack and let cool completely. Finish the pie as directed in the recipe.

to make the dough by hand · In a large bowl, whisk the flour, sugar, and salt until combined. Using a pastry cutter, cut in half the butter, working until it starts to break down. Add the remaining butter and continue cutting it into the flour, until broken down and in various sizes (some butter will be incorporated into the dough, some will still be a bit large, but most should be the size of small peas). Add the egg yolk mixture and, using a spatula, mix until the dough comes together but is still quite shaggy (if the dough is not coming together, add more water 1 tablespoon at a time until it does). Dump the dough out onto a work surface and continue with the directions.

ALL-BUTTER PIE CRUST

Egg yolk and sour cream make for a rich, tender crust, but you can skip them if you want. Omitting them will make a flaky crust that is not as delicate but still easy to roll out. *makes enough for 1 double-crust 9-inch pie*

18 tablespoons (2¼ sticks; 255 g) unsalted butter, cold, cut into 16 to 24 pieces

1 large egg yolk (optional)

1 tablespoon sour cream (optional)

2½ cups (355 g) all-purpose flour

2 tablespoons sugar

1 teaspoon salt

Put the butter in a small bowl and place it in the freezer. Fill a medium liquid measuring cup with water and add plenty of ice. Let both the butter and the ice water sit for 5 to 10 minutes.

In a small liquid measuring cup, combine the egg yolk and sour cream. Pour in some of the very cold water, until all the liquid ingredients together measure ⅓ cup. Whisk together until combined. (If not using the egg yolk and sour cream, just add the water to the dry ingredients.)

In the bowl of a stand mixer fitted with a paddle, mix the flour, sugar, and salt on low until combined. Add half of the chilled butter and mix on low until the butter is just starting to break down, about 1 minute. Add the rest of the butter and continue mixing until the butter is broken down and in various sizes (some butter will be incorporated into the dough, some will still be a bit large, but most should be about the size of small peas). Stop the mixer and use your hands to check for any large pieces of butter that didn't get mixed or any dry patches of dough on the bottom of the bowl; break up the butter and incorporate the dry flour as best you can. With the mixer running on low slowly add the sour cream mixture and mix until the dough starts to come together but still is quite shaggy (if the dough is not coming together, add more water, 1 tablespoon at a time, until it does).

Dump the dough out on a lightly floured work surface and flatten it slightly into a square. Gather any loose/dry pieces that won't stick to the dough and place them on top of the square. Gently fold the dough over onto itself and flatten again. Repeat this process 3 or 4 more times, until all the loose pieces are worked into the dough. Be very gentle with your movements, being careful not to overwork the dough. Flatten the dough one last time into a rectangle and cut into 2 equal pieces. Form the pieces into 6-inch discs and wrap in plastic wrap and refrigerate for 30 minutes before using.

CONTINUED

lattice pie crust · if making a lattice crust or slab pie, use 3 cups (426 g) of flour instead of 2½ cups (355 g). Follow the recipe as written.

whole wheat pie crust · Swap ½ cup (78 g) whole wheat flour for the same amount of white flour. The pie crust will not be quite as flaky as when made with all white flour.

vegan pie crust · Use 1 cup (190 g) shortening or refined coconut oil (extra-virgin oil can give off a coconut-y flavor) in place of the butter, making sure the coconut oil is solid if using (if your coconut oil is very soft or liquidy, you can place it in the fridge until it firms up).

NOTE: *To make the dough by hand,* in a large bowl, whisk the flour, sugar, and salt until combined. Using a pastry cutter, cut in half the butter, working until it starts to break down. Add the remaining butter and continue cutting it into the flour, until broken down and in various sizes (some butter will be incorporated into the dough, some will still be a bit large, but most should be the size of small peas). Add the cream-water mixture and, using a spatula, mix until the dough comes together but is still quite shaggy (if the dough is not coming together, add more water 1 tablespoon at a time until it does). Dump the dough out onto a work surface and continue with the directions.

LATTICE CRUST

Follow the directions for making lattice double-crust pie dough. Lightly flour a work surface, and roll one disc of dough to a 12-inch circle. Gently fold the dough in quarters and place it in the pie plate. Unfold the dough, letting the excess dough drape over the edges. Gently press the dough into the bottom and trim the overhang to 1 inch past the lip. Place the pie plate in the fridge until ready to use.

Line a baking sheet with parchment paper. Lightly flour a work surface and roll out the second disc of dough into a large rectangle ¼ inch thick, and about 18 by 12 inches. You can cut the lattice pieces into any size you'd like; I like a large lattice and cut mine 2¼ to 2½ inches wide. Because I use wide pieces, I cut only 7 strips of lattice, using four vertically and three horizontally. Place the cut strips on the prepared sheet pan and chill in the refrigerator 10 to 15 minutes before using.

When ready to assemble the pie, remove the pie plate and baking sheet from the fridge. Fill the pie as directed in the recipe. Place 4 lattice strips next to one another on

CONTINUED

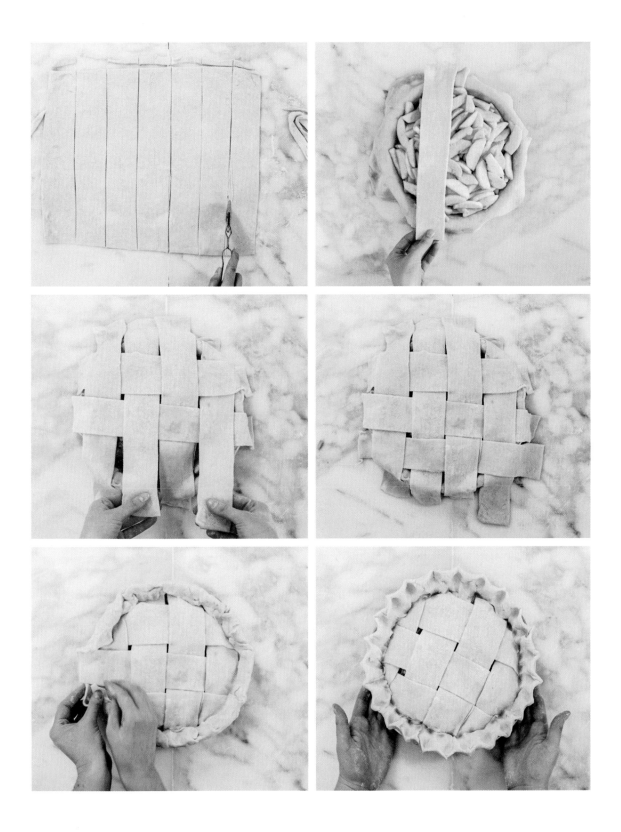

the filling. Weave the remaining 3 lattice strips, lifting the pieces as needed. Trim the overhanging bottom dough to ¾ inch past the lip of the pie plate. Trim the overhanging lattice pieces so they are about ½ inch past the lip. Fold the bottom dough up and over the ends of the lattice strips, creating a rim. Press the dough firmly to lock it in place and then crimp the edge using your fingers (see facing page).

DOUBLE-CRUST

Follow the directions for making double-crust pie dough. Lightly flour a work surface, and roll one disc of dough to a 12-inch circle. Gently fold the dough in quarters and place it in the pie plate. Unfold the dough, letting the excess dough drape over the edges. Gently press the dough into the bottom and trim the overhang to 1 inch past the lip. Place the pie plate in the fridge until ready to use.

Lightly flour a work surface and roll out the second disc of dough into a 12-inch circle. Fold it gently into quarters.

When ready to assemble the pie, remove the pie plate from the fridge and fill as directed in the recipe. Gently unfold the top crust over the filling. Trim the overhang to 1 inch past the lip of the pie plate. Pinch the overhanging top and bottom dough together and then tuck the edge under itself. Crimp the edge with your fingers (see facing page).

GALETTE DOUGH

To make Galette Dough, I use the fraisage method. *Fraisage* is a French approach that requires the dough to be smeared across the work surface, forming long strands of butter in the dough. As it bakes, the thin sheets of butter create a perfectly flaky crust that will hold up to any juicy fruit baked inside. I've tried other techniques, but they always leave the bottom crust soggy. Once you try fraisage, you'll find it works every time! *makes enough for one 9-inch galette, or four 4-inch galettes*

9 tablespoons (128 g) unsalted butter, room temperature, cut into 8 to 10 pieces

1½ cups (213 g) all-purpose flour

1 tablespoon sugar

½ teaspoon salt

Put the butter in a small bowl and place it in the freezer. Fill a medium liquid measuring cup with water and add plenty of ice. Let both the butter and the ice water sit 5 to 10 minutes.

Place the flour, sugar, and salt in the bowl of a food processor fitted with the steel blade. Add the butter and pulse until the size of small peas, 8 to 10 pulses. Add the ice water, 1 tablespoon at a time through the feed tube, and process after each addition until dough holds together when pinched; you'll need 2 to 6 tablespoons of water.

TO FRAISAGE THE DOUGH

Dump out the dough onto a lightly floured surface and pat it into a rectangular-shaped pile. Using the heel of your hand, firmly smear long strips of dough away from you and across the work surface. Continue to smear until the entire pile of dough has been worked, stacking the pieces that form into another pile as you go (see facing page). Collect the smeared dough and move it back to its starting point and repeat the process, smearing the dough away from you using the heel of your hand. The dough should now be cohesive. Gather the dough and form it into a 6-inch disc. Wrap the dough in plastic and refrigerate for 1 hour or up to 2 days.

VARIATION

spelt dough · Replace the 1½ cups (213 g) all-purpose flour with 1¼ cups (179 g) all-purpose flour and ¼ cup (25 g) spelt flour for a mildly flavored spelt dough.

STRAIGHT-UP APPLE PIE

One chilly November afternoon in my mid-twenties, I decided to make a pie for the first time. I had watched my mom make plenty of them over the years; occasionally helping her peel apples or crack open a can of blueberry filling, but I never had completed the process from start to finish by my lonesome, with dough from scratch and a fresh fruit filling. Settling on a recipe, I read through it several times, nervous about keeping the butter cold, rolling perfect circles, and towering the apples high enough. But the kitchen gods smiled upon me, and my dough rolled out like a dream; a perfect covering for my Galas. I made beautiful slashes in the top for steam, brushed the egg wash on with a confident hand, and sent my pie off to the oven. I had done it, taught myself in one try. It came out of the oven over an hour later, with a flaky golden top and a perfectly cooked apple filling. Sure of my pie making abilities, I set out the next week to make another one.

This time around, however, my dough stuck to the counter and cracked at the edges. My rolling pin was my worst enemy, leaving holes and rips wherever it touched. I patched things and I cursed. I angrily mounded apples, but there never seemed to be enough. Regardless, into the oven it went and then out it came: a heap of undercooked apples, with a top crust baked to a crisp and a soggy bottom base. Throughout the years I've had some less-than-perfect pie outcomes, but I'm happy I ended up sticking with pies. I've come to love baking—and eating—them, and find pies worth all the effort. *makes 6 to 8 servings*

1 recipe All-Butter Pie Crust
  (page 187)

8 heaping cups (1,135 g) sliced Gala
  apples (peeled, cored, and sliced
  into ¼-inch pieces), 7 to 8 apples

1 teaspoon lemon juice

⅓ cup (66 g) packed brown sugar

¼ teaspoon salt

¼ cup (50 g) granulated sugar plus
  1 to 2 tablespoons for sprinkling

½ cup apple cider

1 tablespoon (15 g) unsalted butter

1 tablespoon brandy (optional)

1 teaspoon pure vanilla extract

2 tablespoons cornstarch

¾ teaspoon ground cinnamon

½ teaspoon ground ginger

¼ teaspoon grated nutmeg

Egg wash (page 14)

CONTINUED

Combine the apples, lemon juice, brown sugar, and salt in a large bowl. Let sit 1 to 2 hours. While the fruit is macerating, take the All-Butter Pie Crust out of the refrigerator and let come to room temperature. Strain the sugary juice from the fruit into a medium saucepan (you should have ½ to ¾ cup of juice). Return the apples to the large bowl.

Add the granulated sugar and cider to the saucepan and bring to a boil over medium heat. Simmer until reduced to a scant ½ cup, 5 to 6 minutes, shaking the pan occasionally to stir. Remove from the heat and whisk in the butter. Add the brandy (if using) and vanilla and stir gently.

Sprinkle the cornstarch over the apples and toss to coat. Add the cinnamon, ginger, and nutmeg and toss to combine. Pour the apple juice mixture over the fruit and stir gently.

TO ASSEMBLE AND BAKE: Lightly flour a work surface and roll the dough into a 12-inch circle about ¼ inch thick and place it into a 9-inch pie plate. Transfer the plate to the fridge and let chill while you roll out the second piece of dough. On a lightly floured work surface, roll the second piece of dough into a 12-inch circle, about ¼ thick. Set aside.

Fill the prepared pie shell with the apple mixture and top with the second crust. Trim the dough overhangs to 1 inch past the lip of the pie plate. Pinch the dough together and tuck it under itself so it's resting on the edge of the pie plate. Crimp the edges of the dough and cut at least 4 vents in the top, each about 2 inches long (see page 194). Transfer the pie plate to the freezer for about 20 minutes while the oven is preheating. The crust should be nice and firm before you bake it.

Adjust an oven rack to the lowest position. Preheat oven to 425°F. Place a baking sheet on the oven rack (the preheated baking sheet helps crisp the bottom of the pie crust and also catches any leaks and drips).

When ready to bake, brush the top with egg wash and sprinkle with 1 or 2 tablespoons of granulated sugar. Transfer the pie plate to the preheated baking sheet and bake 25 minutes. Reduce the oven to 375°F and bake 40 to 50 minutes, until the crust is deep golden brown and the juices bubble.

Transfer the pie plate to a wire rack and let cool at least 4 hours before serving.

NOTE: The cider adds a lot of apple flavor to this pie, but it can be omitted. Let the apples macerate for 2 hours and cook the strained juice with the granulated sugar as directed until it is a scant ½ cup. Proceed with the recipe. Hard cider can also be used instead of the regular cider.

PEACH-CARAMEL PIE

❧❦

When I was growing up, a few weekends a year my family would take a trip to visit my grandma Ethel. The car ride was long, and we were usually tired and cranky on arrival, but as soon as she opened the door in welcome, we couldn't all help but smile. A waft of kitchen goodness would hit us instantly: roast chicken, mashed potatoes and gravy, fresh baked bread, and pie. There were always three or four homemade pies sitting out on her counter, still slightly warm. After eating our meal we would beg for a piece, and while my siblings stuck with apple and my dad settled on blueberry, I always eagerly devoured a slice of peach.

In this recipe, I've mimicked her flaky crust and juicy peach filling. She never kept a record of what went in her pies, so I took the liberty of expanding on my memory. Here the peach juice is cooked down along with sugar, and a little butter and heavy cream are added to make a caramel-like sauce that is stirred into the fruit. Peach schnapps and a hint of cinnamon add a nice flavor boost, and the all-butter crust makes each bite a comfort-food masterpiece. *makes 6 to 8 servings*

1 recipe All-Butter Pie Crust (page 187)

8 cups (1,135 g) sliced peaches, ripe but still firm (peeled, pitted, and sliced into 1-inch pieces), 7 to 8 peaches

1 cup (150 g) peeled and grated Gala apple, about 2 small apples

½ cup (99 g) sugar, plus ¼ cup (50 g) and 1 to 2 tablespoons for sprinkling

¼ teaspoon salt

2 tablespoons (29 g) unsalted butter, cold

2 tablespoons heavy cream

2 tablespoons peach schnapps (optional)

1 teaspoon pure vanilla extract

¼ cup (28 g) cornstarch

1 teaspoon lemon juice

½ teaspoon ground cinnamon

Egg wash (page 14)

Combine the peaches, apple, ½ cup sugar, and salt in a large bowl. Let sit 30 to 45 minutes at room temperature. While the fruit is macerating, take the All-Butter Pie Crust out of the refrigerator and let it come to room temperature.

Strain the sugary juice from the fruit into a medium saucepan (you should have ½ to ¾ cup of juice). Return the fruit to the large bowl.

Add the remaining ¼ cup of sugar to the saucepan and bring to a boil over medium heat. Simmer until reduced to a scant ½ cup, 5 to 6 minutes, shaking the

CONTINUED

pan occasionally to stir. Remove from the heat and whisk in the butter. Add the heavy cream, peach schnapps (if using), and vanilla and stir gently. Set aside to cool slightly.

Sprinkle the cornstarch over the fruit and toss to coat. Add the lemon juice and cinnamon and toss to combine. Pour the peach juice mixture over the fruit and stir gently.

TO ASSEMBLE AND BAKE: Lightly flour a work surface and roll out one piece of the dough into a 12-inch circle about ¼ inch thick and place it into a 9-inch pie plate. Transfer the plate to the fridge and let chill while you roll out the second piece of dough. On a lightly floured work surface, roll out the other piece of dough into a 12-inch circle about ¼ inch thick. Set aside.

Fill the prepared pie shell with the peach mixture. It will be juicy, and if some of the filling starts to ooze over the edge, use a measuring cup to scoop out ½ cup or so, and omit it. Top with the second crust. Trim the dough overhangs to 1 inch past the lip of the pie plate. Pinch the dough together and tuck it under itself so it's resting on the edge of the pie plate. Crimp the edges of the dough and cut at least four vents in the top, each about 2 inches long (see photos on page 190). Place the pie plate into the freezer for about 20 minutes while the oven is preheating. The crust should be nice and firm before you bake it.

Adjust an oven rack to the lowest position. Preheat the oven to 425°F. Place a baking sheet on the oven rack (the preheated baking sheet helps crisp the bottom of the pie crust and also catches any leaks and drips).

When ready to bake, brush the top of the pie with egg wash and sprinkle with 1 or 2 tablespoons of sugar. Transfer the pie to the preheated baking sheet and bake 25 minutes. Reduce the oven to 375°F and bake 40 to 50 minutes, until the crust is deep golden brown and the juices bubble.

Transfer the pie plate to a wire rack and cool at least 4 hours before serving.

NOTES: Ripe but still firm peaches can be peeled easily with a vegetable peeler.

The filling can occasionally ooze over the edge of the bottom crust when filling it. This can happen if the peaches are extra ripe, or the peach juice mixture hasn't been boiled down enough.

You do not have to add the peach schnapps, but I like the extra bump of peach flavor it gives the pie.

PEAR-APPLE HARD CIDER PIE

Nigel Slater describes an apple in his book *Ripe* as a "quick hit," but the pear as "something to take our time over." I would have to agree and have always been partial to pears over apples, especially when it comes to pies. Here, however, I've combined them; this pie is chockfull of fresh pears, and their juice is cooked down with a good splash of hard apple cider. It's a fantastic combination, a perfect pie for crisp autumn evenings and then for breakfast the following morning. *makes 6 to 8 servings*

1 recipe All-Butter Pie Crust (page 187)

8 cups (1,135 g) sliced Bartlett pears, ripe, but still firm (peeled, cored, and sliced into 1-inch pieces), 7 to 8 pears

1 cup (150 g) peeled and grated Gala apple, about 2 small apples

1 teaspoon lemon juice

⅓ cup (66 g) sugar plus ¼ cup (50 g) plus 1 to 2 tablespoons for sprinkling

¼ teaspoon salt

½ cup hard apple cider (regular apple cider will work, too)

1 tablespoon (15 g) unsalted butter, cold

1 teaspoon pure vanilla extract

3 tablespoons cornstarch

½ teaspoon ground cinnamon

¼ teaspoon grated nutmeg

⅛ teaspoon ground cloves

Egg wash (page 14)

Combine the pears, apple, lemon juice, ⅓ cup sugar, and salt in a large bowl. Let sit 30 to 45 minutes at room temperature. While the fruit is macerating, take the All-Butter Pie Crust out of the refrigerator and let it come to room temperature. Strain the sugary juice from the fruit into a medium saucepan (you should have ½ to ¾ cup of juice). Return the fruit to the large bowl.

Add the remaining ¼ cup sugar and cider to the saucepan and bring to a boil over medium heat. Simmer until reduced to a scant ½ cup, 5 to 6 minutes, shaking the pan occasionally to stir. Remove from the heat and whisk in the butter. Add the vanilla and stir gently. Set aside to cool slightly.

Sprinkle the cornstarch over the fruit and toss to coat. Add the cinnamon, nutmeg, and cloves and toss to combine. Pour the apple-pear juice mixture over the fruit and stir gently.

CONTINUED

TO ASSEMBLE AND BAKE: Lightly flour a work surface and roll the dough into a 12-inch circle about ¼-inch thick and place it into a 9-inch pie pan. Transfer the plate in the fridge and let chill while you roll out the second piece of dough. On a lightly floured work surface, roll out the second piece of dough into a 12-inch circle about ¼ inch thick. Set aside.

Fill the prepared pie shell with the pear mixture. It will be juicy, and if some of the filling starts to ooze over the edge, use a measuring cup to scoop out ½ cup or so, and omit it. Top with the second crust. Trim the dough overhangs to 1 inch past the lip of the pie plate. Pinch the dough together and tuck it under itself so it's resting on the edge of the pie plate. Crimp the edges of the dough and cut at least 4 vents in the top, each about 2 inches long. Transfer the pie plate to the freezer for about 20 minutes while the oven is preheating. The crust should be nice and firm before you bake it.

Adjust an oven rack to the lowest position. Preheat the oven to 425°F. Place a baking sheet on the oven rack (the preheated baking sheet helps crisp the bottom of the pie crust and catches any leaks and drips).

When ready to bake, brush the top of the pie with egg wash and sprinkle with 1 to 2 tablespoons of granulated sugar. Place the pie plate on the preheated baking sheet and bake 25 minutes. Lower the oven to 375°F and bake 40 to 50 minutes, until the crust is deep golden brown and the juices bubble.

Transfer the pie plate to a wire rack and let cool at least 4 hours before serving.

NOTES: Your favorite hard cider will work here. I prefer a dry hard cider (Crispin makes a tasty one) in this pie. Regular apple cider will work just fine too.

STRAWBERRY-CHERRY SLAB PIE

While reading through piles of books on pies, one piece of advice I frequently came across was to never make a strawberry or sweet cherry pie, noting that it would turn out both too mushy and too sweet. In a fit of rebellion, I created this recipe, which combines both fruits and allows them a moment to shine. This is a pie for midsummer, in rectangle form. Its flaky outer crust and sweet, delicious filling make it a great choice to bring to picnics, BBQs, and the Fourth of July to feed a crowd. *makes 10 to 12 servings*

1 recipe All-Butter Pie Crust slab pie variation (page 187)

5 cups (1½ pounds/680 g) pitted sweet cherries

4 cups (1 pound/600 g) hulled strawberries, quartered

1 cup (150 g) peeled and grated Gala apple, about 2 small apples

½ cup (99 g) sugar plus ¼ cup (50 g) plus 1 to 2 tablespoons for sprinkling

¼ teaspoon salt

2 tablespoons (29 g) unsalted butter

1 tablespoon kirsch (optional)

1 teaspoon pure vanilla extract

¼ cup (28 g) cornstarch

1 teaspoon lemon juice

⅛ teaspoon ground cinnamon

1 vanilla bean, seeds scraped (optional)

Egg wash (page 14)

Combine the cherries, strawberries, apple, ½ cup sugar, and salt in a large bowl. Let sit 30 to 45 minutes at room temperature. While the fruit is macerating, take the All-Butter Pie Crust out of the refrigerator and let it come to room temperature. Strain the sugary juice into a medium saucepan (you should have ½ to ¾ cup of juice). Return the fruit to the large bowl.

Add the remaining ¼ cup sugar to the saucepan with the juice and bring to a boil over medium heat. Simmer until reduced to a scant ½ cup, 5 to 6 minutes, shaking the pan occasionally to stir. Remove from the heat and whisk in the butter. Add the kirsch (if using) and vanilla and whisk again. Set aside to cool slightly.

Sprinkle the cornstarch over the fruit and toss to coat. Add the lemon juice, cinnamon, and vanilla bean seeds (if using) and toss to combine. Pour the strawberry-cherry juice mixture over the fruit and stir gently.

CONTINUED

TO ASSEMBLE AND BAKE: Lightly flour a large sheet of parchment paper, and roll one piece of dough into a 17 by 13-inch rectangle. Repeat with the second piece of dough. Using the parchment paper, transfer one rectangle to a 13 by 9-inch jelly roll pan or quarter sheet pan. Press the dough into the pan; discard the parchment. Pour the filling on top of the dough and spread into an even layer. Using the parchment paper, place the second rectangle of dough on top of the filling; discard the parchment. Trim the dough overhangs to 1 inch past the lip of the pan. Pinch the dough together and tuck it under itself. Crimp the edges and cut several X-shaped vents across the top of the dough. Place the pan in the freezer for about 20 minutes while the oven is preheating. You want the crust to be nice and firm before you bake it.

Adjust an oven rack to the lowest position. Preheat oven to 425°F. Place a baking sheet large enough to hold the jelly roll pan on the oven rack (the preheated baking sheet helps crisp the bottom of the pie crust and catches any leaks and drips).

When you are ready to bake, brush the top of the pie evenly with egg wash and sprinkle with 1 or 2 tablespoons of granulated sugar. Put the jelly roll pan on the preheated baking sheet and bake 25 minutes. Reduce the oven to 375°F and bake 40 to 50 minutes, until the crust is deep golden brown and the juices bubble.

Transfer the jelly roll pan to a wire rack and let cool at least 4 hours before serving.

VARIATION

cherry slab pie · Omit the strawberries and use 2½ pounds (1,135 g) pitted sweet cherries.

NOTE: Kirsch is a clear cherry brandy that is not sweet. It gives nice flavor to this pie, but can be omitted.

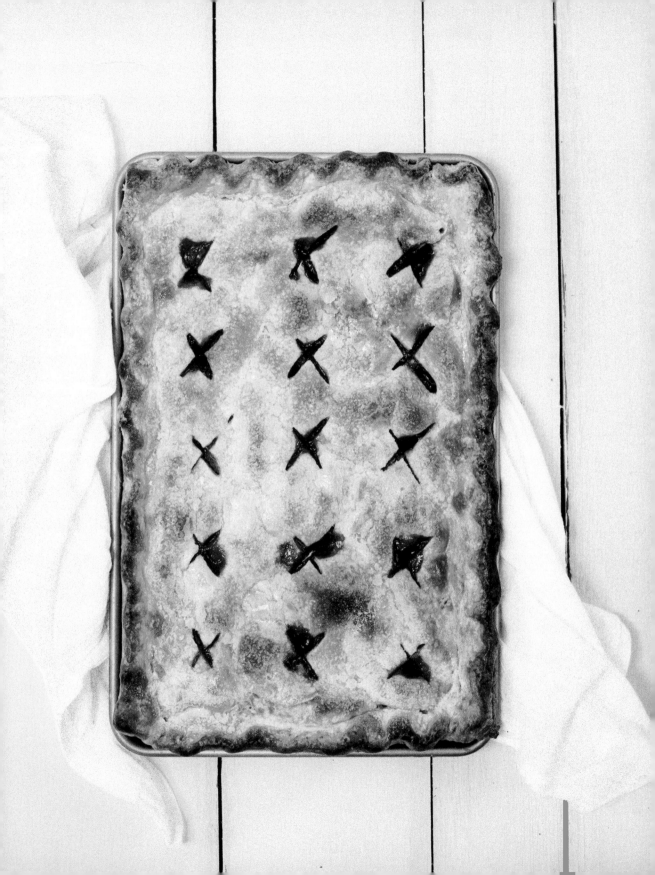

BERRY CREAM PIE

In high school, just before discovering how delicious iced mochas were, I went through a French soda phase. French sodas are a cold drink made with a sweet flavored syrup, carbonated water, a splash of cream, and more often than not, an extravagant pile of whipped cream. I often ordered these in berry flavors and sipped them in coffee shops with friends after school. This pie recalls those afternoons, and the berry-and-cream filling served with a hearty helping of whipped cream is similar in flavor to those sweet, delicious drinks. I like to make this pie in the summer when berries are at their prime. *makes 6 to 8 servings*

1 recipe All-Butter Pie Crust (page 187)

3 cups (420 g) blueberries

2 cups (300 g) quartered strawberries

2 cups (340 g) raspberries

1 cup (170 g) blackberries

1 cup (150 g) peeled and grated Gala apple, about 2 small apples

½ cup (99 g) sugar plus ¼ cup (50 g), plus 1 to 2 tablespoons for sprinkling

¼ teaspoon salt

1 tablespoon (15 g) unsalted butter, cold

¼ cup heavy cream

2 teaspoons pure vanilla extract

¼ cup (28 g) cornstarch

1 tablespoon lemon juice

½ teaspoon ground cinnamon

Egg wash (page 14)

Combine the berries, apple, ½ cup sugar, and salt in a large bowl. Let sit 30 to 45 minutes at room temperature. While the fruit is macerating, take the All-Butter Pie Crust out of the refrigerator and let it come to room temperature.

Strain the sugary juice from the fruit into a medium saucepan (you should have ½ to ¾ cup of juice). Return the fruit to the large bowl.

Add the remaining ¼ cup of sugar to the saucepan and bring to a boil over medium heat. Simmer until reduced to a scant ½ cup, 5 to 6 minutes, shaking the pan occasionally to stir. Remove from the heat and whisk in the butter. Add the heavy cream and vanilla and stir gently. Set aside to cool slightly.

Sprinkle the cornstarch over the berries and toss to coat. Add the lemon juice and cinnamon and toss to combine. Pour the cream mixture over the fruit and stir gently.

TO ASSEMBLE AND BAKE: Lightly flour a work surface; roll out one piece of the dough into a 12-inch circle about ¼ inch thick, and place it into a 9-inch pie plate. Place the plate in the fridge and let chill while you roll out the second piece of dough. On a lightly floured work surface, roll out the second piece of dough into a 12-inch circle about ¼ thick. Set aside.

Fill the prepared pie shell with the berry mixture. It will be juicy, and if some of the filling starts to ooze over the edge, use a measuring cup to scoop out ½ cup or so, and omit it. Top with the second crust. Trim the dough overhangs to 1 inch past the lip of the pie plate. Pinch the dough together, and tuck it under itself so it's resting on the edge of the pie plate. Crimp the edges of the dough and cut at least 4 vents in the top, each about 2 inches long. Place the pie plate in the freezer for about 20 minutes while the oven is preheating. The crust should be nice and firm before you bake it.

Adjust an oven rack to the lowest position. Preheat the oven to 425°F. Place a baking sheet on the oven rack (the preheated baking sheet helps crisp the bottom of the pie crust and catches any leaks and drips).

When ready to bake, brush the top of the pie with egg wash and sprinkle with 1 or 2 tablespoons of granulated sugar. Put the pie plate on the preheated baking sheet and bake 25 minutes. Reduce the oven to 375°F and bake 40 to 50 minutes, until the crust is deep golden brown and the juices bubble.

Transfer the pie plate to a wire rack and let cool at least 4 hours before serving.

PHOTOGRAPH ON PAGE 178

APPLE-GINGER SKILLET PIE

There are days when there just isn't enough time to make a double-crust pie. That's when skillet pie becomes your ally. Apples, ginger, sugar, spice, and a layer of puff pastry all have the right moves. They bake together to become a juicy, flaky goodness that is easily passed off as pie. No one will know the difference, especially when served with a generous topping of Whipped Cream (page 306) or Pumpkin No-Churn Ice Cream (page 287). *makes 6 to 8 servings*

½ recipe Rough Puff Pastry (page 75) or 1 sheet (½ pound) store bought, thawed if frozen

8 heaping cups (1,135 g) sliced Gala apples, peel, cored, and sliced into ¼-inch pieces, 7 to 8 apples

¼ cup (50 g) sugar, plus ¼ cup (50 g), and more for dusting

1 teaspoon lemon juice

2 tablespoons cornstarch

¾ teaspoon ground ginger

¼ teaspoon ground cinnamon

¾ cup hard cider or apple cider

1 tablespoon grated fresh gingerroot

¼ teaspoon salt

1 tablespoon (15 g) unsalted butter, cold

½ teaspoon pure vanilla extract

Adjust an oven rack to the lower middle position. Preheat the oven to 400°F.

Place the apples, ¼ cup sugar, lemon juice, cornstarch, ground ginger, and cinnamon in a large bowl and toss to combine.

In a medium saucepan over medium heat bring the cider, ¼ cup sugar, fresh ginger, and salt to a boil. Cook until reduced to a scant ½ cup. Remove from the heat and stir in the butter and vanilla.

Pour the apple cider mixture over the apples and stir gently. Pour the apples and all the juices into a 10-inch ovenproof skillet and press into an even layer. Bake 12 minutes, until the apples are slightly tender.

While the apples are baking, cut the puff pastry into a scant 10-inch circle (you want it to fit just inside the skillet). Cut an X in the middle of the puff pastry and refrigerate until ready to use.

After 12 minutes, carefully remove the skillet from the oven. Place the puff pastry over the top of the apples (remember, the pan is hot). Brush the top of the pastry with water and then sprinkle with a generous dusting of sugar. Return the skillet to the oven and bake 20 to 22 minutes, until the puff pastry is puffed and deep golden and the juices underneath are bubbling.

Transfer to a wire rack and let cool 10 minutes before serving.

NOTES: I like Gala apples here, but your favorite baking apple will work just fine. I prefer a sweeter apple paired with the gingerroot.

Hard cider or apple cider is called for, but in a pinch apple juice or even water can be substituted (although, the pie won't have quite as much apple flavor).

CHOCOLATE MERINGUE PIE

I'm pretty sure this pie doesn't need me to make a case for it. The crust is thin and golden and crisp, a perfect little bed for the rich chocolate filling. Meringue is gently spooned on top, a toasted marshmallow-like tower. It is worth every second spent over the stove, and every whirl and whisk of the mixer. *serves 6 to 8*

1 recipe Single-Crust Pie Dough (page 183), fully baked and cooled

CHOCOLATE FILLING

½ cup heavy cream

7 ounces (199 g) bittersweet chocolate, melted and cooled

4 large eggs

¾ cup (149 g) granulated sugar

¼ cup (50 g) packed brown sugar

¼ teaspoon salt

3 tablespoons coffee or water, room temperature

2 teaspoons pure vanilla extract

8 tablespoons (1 stick; 113 g) unsalted butter, room temperature and cut into pieces

MERINGUE

5 large egg whites

1 cup (198 g) sugar

¼ teaspoon salt

2 teaspoons pure vanilla extract

FOR THE FILLING: In the bowl of a stand mixer fitted with the whisk, beat the heavy cream on low speed until small bubbles form, about 30 seconds. Increase the speed to high and continue beating until the cream is smooth, thick, and nearly double in volume, about 30 seconds. Transfer the whipped cream to a bowl and place it in the refrigerator. Clean the mixing bowl if you have only one.

Put about 1 inch of water in a medium saucepan and bring to a gentle boil. Melt the chocolate in a heatproof bowl set over the pan of boiling water, being careful not to let the water touch the bottom of the bowl. Stir constantly until just melted and set aside to cool. Add more water to the saucepan if needed, and bring to a boil again.

In the (clean) bowl of a stand mixer, stir the eggs, sugars, salt, and coffee to combine. Place the bowl over the saucepan, being careful not to let the water touch the bottom of the bowl. Stir with a rubber spatula until the sugar is completely melted and reaches a temperature of 160°F, 4 to 5 minutes. While you are stirring, be sure to scrape down the sides of the bowl with the spatula—this will ensure no sugar grains are lurking on the sides and will help prevent the eggs from cooking.

CONTINUED

Remove the bowl from the heat and place it in the stand mixer fitted with a whisk. Whisk on high until light and fluffy, 8 to 10 minutes. The bowl should have cooled down to room temperature at this point. Switch to the paddle attachment, add the chocolate and vanilla, and beat on low until combined. With the mixer running on medium, add a few pieces of butter at a time, beating until completely incorporated. Remove the bowl from the mixer and, using a spatula, gently fold in the chilled whipped cream.

Pour the filling into the prepared pie crust and use an offset spatula to even out the top. Move the pie to the refrigerator, and cover the top of the pie with a piece of parchment paper to keep off condensation. Let the pie chill at least 4 hours, or overnight. When ready to serve, top with the meringue.

FOR THE MERINGUE: Put about an inch of water in a medium saucepan and bring it to a gentle boil.

In the bowl of a stand mixer, stir the egg whites, sugar, and salt to combine. Put the bowl over the saucepan, being careful not to let the water touch the bottom of the bowl. Stir with a rubber spatula until the sugar is completely melted and reaches a temperature of 160°F, 4 to 5 minutes. While you are stirring, be sure to scrape down the sides of the bowl with the spatula—this will ensure no sugar grains are lurking on the sides and will help prevent the egg whites from cooking.

Remove the bowl from the heat and place it in the stand mixer fitted with a whisk. Whisk on medium-high until stiff, glossy peaks form, 8 to 10 minutes. The bowl should have cooled down to room temperature at this point. Add the vanilla and beat on low until combined.

Take the chilled pie from the refrigerator, and remove the parchment paper. Working quickly, use a spatula to spread the meringue over the top of the pie. Use a spoon to create curls and peaks in the meringue. Hold a kitchen blowtorch 1 to 2 inches away from the meringue and touch the flame down in between the curls. The curls will toast and brown (if the curls set on fire, you can blow them out). Do this until you are happy with the color.

If you do not have a torch, you can brown the meringue under a broiler. Adjust your oven rack so the pie will be a few inches below the broiler. Preheat the broiler. Place the pie on a baking sheet and place the sheet under the broiler until the tips of the meringue curls begin to brown, turning the baking sheet as needed. Because the pie is chilled, it is important to take it out of the oven as quickly as possible so the filling doesn't melt. The meringue is best served within a few hours; it will begin to weep after about twelve.

ORANGE PIE

One day I had set out to make Key lime pie, only to discover I didn't have enough limes on hand. But there were plenty of oranges in the bottom drawer of my refrigerator, so I made an even trade, orange for green. The pie was not as tart, of course, but still lush and creamy. It was so good I made it again, this time topping it with a mound of orange-flavored whipped cream studded with vanilla bean seeds. In January and February, I like to make it with blood oranges; their tart juice adds a little different flavor. *makes 6 to 8 servings*

CRUST

1½ cups (150 g) graham cracker crumbs (or 11 whole graham crackers pulsed in a food processor)

3 tablespoons sugar

5 tablespoons (72 g) unsalted butter, melted and cooled

FILLING

4 large egg yolks

2 tablespoons heavy cream

½ cup orange juice

1 tablespoon lemon juice

1 teaspoon pure vanilla extract

¼ teaspoon salt

One 14-ounce can (396 g) sweetened condensed milk

1 to 2 drops orange food coloring (optional)

WHIPPED CREAM

4 ounces (113 g) cream cheese, room temperature

2 tablespoons sugar

2 tablespoons triple sec

1 teaspoon pure vanilla extract

1 teaspoon grated orange zest

1 vanilla bean, seeds scraped (optional)

Pinch salt

1½ cups heavy cream

FOR THE CRUST: Adjust an oven rack to the middle position. Preheat the oven to 325°F.

In a medium bowl, combine the graham cracker crumbs and sugar. Add the butter and stir until well blended. Using a measuring cup or spoon, press the crumbs evenly on the bottom and up the sides of a 9-inch pie plate. Bake 12 to 15 minutes, until lightly browned and fragrant.

Transfer the pie pan to a wire rack and let cool slightly.

CONTINUED

FOR THE FILLING: In a large bowl, whisk the yolks, heavy cream, orange juice, lemon juice, vanilla, salt, and sweetened condensed milk until smooth and fully combined. Add the food coloring, if using, and whisk until evenly incorporated.

Pour the filling into the warm pie crust and return the pie plate to the oven. Bake 14 to 17 minutes, until the center is set but still a bit wiggly when jiggled.

Transfer the pie plate to a wire rack and let cool completely. Refrigerate until well chilled, at least 4 hours or overnight. Before serving, top it with the orange whipped cream.

FOR THE WHIPPED CREAM: In the bowl of a stand mixer fitted with a paddle, beat the cream cheese on medium until smooth. Add the sugar, triple sec, vanilla, orange zest, vanilla bean seeds, and salt. Beat on low until combined, then increase the speed to medium and beat until smooth. Scrape down the sides of the bowl and switch to the whisk. With the mixer running on low, slowly add the heavy cream and whisk until fully combined. Increase the speed to medium and beat until stiff peaks form, stopping to scrape down the sides of the bowl as needed, 2 to 3 minutes.

NOTE: If you are using blood oranges, you may need to use 1 or 2 drops of orange food coloring because the purple juice will make the filling look an odd color when baked.

CHERRY-RHUBARB CRISP
WITH WHITE WINE

Rhubarb is an important plant to all Minnesotans. Not only can it be found in nearly every neighbor's garden and growing alongside walking paths and trails in local parks but for those of us living North, it is also a symbol of winter's end. As its green leaves and pink stalks start to peek out of the ground, there is a collective sigh of relief among us all. The winter has come and gone. Spring is here, at last.

I've eaten many rhubarb crisps in my day that have been either a mouth-puckering affair or a soggy pile saturated in sugar. But I've also tasted some incredible rhubarb pies, tarts, and even ice cream over the years, and I knew there was hope for this plant in my kitchen. After some experimenting, I found that including sweet cherries alongside helps balance the sharp flavor of the rhubarb, without having to add extra sweeteners that often make the dessert cloying. The topping adds needed crunch, and a scoop of Vanilla No-Churn Ice Cream (page 277) rounds out the flavors nicely.

makes 6 to 8 servings

¼ cup (28 g) cornstarch

¼ cup (50 g) sugar, plus ½ cup (99 g) sugar

⅛ teaspoon cinnamon

1 cup sweet white wine

1 vanilla bean, scraped

¼ teaspoon salt

6 cups (680 g) sweet cherries

3½ cups (1 pound, 454 g) sliced rhubarb (cut into 1-inch pieces)

1 tablespoon (15 g) unsalted butter, room temperature

1 teaspoon lemon juice

WHOLE WHEAT STREUSEL

½ cup (78 g) whole wheat flour

½ cup (71 g) all-purpose flour

½ cup (45 g) rolled oats

¼ cup (50 g) granulated sugar

¼ cup (50 g) packed brown sugar

¼ teaspoon salt

7 tablespoons (101 g) unsalted butter, room temperature

In a small bowl, combine the cornstarch, ¼ cup (50 g) sugar, and cinnamon.

In a large saucepan, combine the white wine, remaining ½ cup (99 g) sugar, vanilla bean seeds, vanilla bean pod, and salt. Bring to a boil over medium-high heat. Add the

CONTINUED

cherries and rhubarb to the saucepan and let them boil for 1 minute. Turn off the heat and add the butter to the fruit, stirring until the butter is melted and combined. Let the mixture cool until slightly warm.

Adjust oven racks to the middle upper and lower positon. Preheat the oven to 400°F. Line a baking sheet with parchment paper.

Prepare the whole wheat streusel. In the bowl of a stand mixer fitted with the paddle, combine the whole wheat and all-purpose flours, granulated and brown sugars, and salt. With the mixer running on low, add the butter, 1 tablespoon at a time, until the mixture comes together but still is quite crumbly. Pour the mixture into the prepared pan in an even layer.

Remove the vanilla bean pod from the cherry-rhubarb mixture and discard. Stir in the lemon juice, then stir in the cornstarch mixture until completely combined.

Pour all the contents from the saucepan into a 9 x 13 baking dish and place in the oven on the upper middle rack. Place the streusel on the lower middle rack. Let the streusel bake for 8 minutes, then remove from the oven and let cool slightly. Let the fruit bake for 10-15 more minutes after the streusel is removed, until the liquid from the fruit begins bubbling at the sides of the dish. Carefully remove the pan from the oven, and top the fruit evenly with the streusel. Bake for 15 to 20 more minutes, until the fruit is soft, the liquid is thick and bubbly, and the streusel is golden brown.

Transfer the baking dish to a wire rack and let the cool slightly before serving. Serve with Whipped Cream (page 306) or ice cream.

PEAR-CHOCOLATE GALETTES

Pears and chocolate work very well together and are a classic combination. The pears are juicy and sweet, the chocolate is rich and deep. Dusted with a sprinkle of cacao nib sugar, this is a lovely dessert for cool autumn evenings, when pears are at their peak. *makes 4 galettes*

1 recipe Galette Dough (page 192)

2 cups (340 g) sliced pears (peeled, cored, and sliced into ¼-inch pieces), 2 to 3 pears

1 tablespoon sugar (see note)

½ teaspoon pure vanilla extract

Pinch salt

1 ounce (29 g) bittersweet chocolate, chopped

Egg wash (page 14)

Cacao Nib Sugar (page 309), for sprinkling

Line a baking sheet with parchment paper.

Divide the Galette Dough into four equal pieces. Lightly flour a work surface and roll each piece into a 6 to 7-inch circle, about ⅛ inch thick. Transfer the rounds to the prepared pan (they may overlap a bit) and put it in the fridge while you prepare the filling.

In a large bowl, combine the pears, sugar, vanilla, and salt.

Remove the pastry from the fridge and divide the chocolate evenly between the circles. Then divide the fruit evenly among the circles, leaving a ¾-inch border around the edges. Fold the edges of the pastry over the filling and pleat it evenly every few inches (see page 220). Chill the formed galettes in the refrigerator while the oven preheats.

Adjust an oven rack to the lower middle position. Preheat the oven to 400°F.

Remove the baking sheet from the fridge, gently brush the pastry with the egg wash and sprinkle generously with the cacao nib sugar. Bake 25 to 30 minutes, until the crusts are deep golden and the juices are bubbling. Move the pan to a wire rack and let the galettes cool on the pan before serving.

NOTE: If your pears are very ripe and sweet, the sugar isn't necessary to add.

You can add extra chocolate to your galettes, but I found less was more in this application.

MIXED BERRY GALETTES

I've always loved making galettes. Pies are homey, cakes are fancy, and galettes fall somewhere in between. They can be rustic or sexy, laid back or all dressed up. Their dainty size gives them a cute factor, but berries topped with crème fraîche makes them a more grown-up affair, perfect for a late-night dinner party dessert. ***makes 4 galettes***

1 recipe Galette Dough (page 192)

2 cups (240 g) mixed berries, any combination of blueberries, raspberries, or blackberries

1 teaspoon lemon juice

½ teaspoon pure vanilla extract

2 tablespoons sugar plus more as needed for sweetness (see note) and for sprinkling

1 tablespoon cornstarch

Pinch salt

¼ cup berry-flavored jam

Egg wash (page 14)

Line a baking sheet with parchment paper.

Divide the Galette Dough into four equal pieces. Lightly flour a work surface and roll each piece into a 6- to 7-inch circle, about ⅛ inch thick. Transfer the circles to the prepared pan (they may overlap a bit) and place it in the fridge while you prepare the filling.

In a large bowl, combine the berries, lemon juice, and vanilla. In a small bowl, combine the sugar, cornstarch, and salt. Add the sugar mixture to the berries and toss gently to combine. Taste the berries. If extra sugar is needed, add 1 to 2 tablespoons more.

Remove the pastry from the fridge and spread each circle with 1 tablespoon of jam, and divide the fruit evenly among the circles, leaving a ¾-inch border around the edges. Fold the edges of the pastry over the filling and pleat it every few inches (see page 220). Chill the formed galettes in the refrigerator while the oven preheats.

Adjust an oven rack to the lower middle position. Preheat the oven to 400°F.

Remove the baking sheet from the fridge and gently brush the pastry with egg wash and sprinkle generously with sugar. Bake 25 to 30 minutes, until the crusts are deep golden and the juices are bubbling. Move the pan to a wire rack and let the galettes cool on the pan before serving.

Serve with Crème Fraîche (page 305), Whipped Cream (page 306), or ice cream.

BANANA CREAM HAND PIES

If I recall any Father's Day from my childhood, I see my dad: eating, laughing, opening up boxes and bags filled with brightly colored ties and random books we were certain he'd be interested in. I also see a Banana Cream Pie from a local chain pie shop sitting on the kitchen counter, its whipped cream top peeping out at us from a red square box. His favorite pie. I've never been able to make a full-size banana cream pie for him that I loved, but these hand pies are so delicious, I may never have to. Bananas are tucked into puff pastry circles and baked until golden brown, then filled with pastry cream and eaten immediately. *makes 10 hand pies*

1 recipe Rough Puff Pastry (page 75)
2 large bananas, cut into ¼-inch slices

½ teaspoon lemon juice
Sugar, for sprinkling
1 cup Pastry Cream (page 310)

In a medium bowl, toss the bananas with the lemon juice.

Line a baking sheet with parchment paper. Place the puff pastry on a floured work surface. Roll the dough into an 18 x 14-inch rectangle, flouring as necessary.

Use a 3½-inch circular biscuit or cookie cutter (the rim of a cup will also work) to cut out 20 circles in the puff pastry. Place 10 circles in the prepared pan. Brush the border of each circle with water, and then place 4 to 5 banana slices in the circle, overlapping them slightly and leaving a bit of a border around the edge of the circle. Place a second dough circle on top of each circle, and press firmly on the edges to adhere. Place the baking sheet in the freezer while the oven preheats.

Adjust the oven rack to the middle position. Preheat the oven to 400°F.

Remove the baking sheet from the freezer, cut a small X in the center of each circle to vent the pastry, and brush the tops lightly with water. Sprinkle the tops generously with sugar.

Bake 14 to 16 minutes, until the pies are golden brown.

Transfer the baking sheet to a wire rack and let them cool completely. Fill a piping bag fitted with a plain tip with the Pastry Cream (a zipper-locking plastic bag with the corner snipped off will also work). Gently push the tip into the vent on top of the hand pies and fill each with a tablespoon or two of pastry cream. These are best eaten the same day.

NOTE: The larger you make the hand pies, the more pastry cream you can fill the insides with. So if you like more of a cream-to-crust ratio, a 5-inch hand pie is a good choice. You will need extra bananas and pastry cream, and will need to add a few minutes to the bake time.

You can use store-bought puff pastry here, but since it is usually sold in 2 sheets, you will not be able to get quite as many circles out of 1 pound.

BLACKBERRY-APRICOT HAND PIES

Hand pies are *almost* better than regular pies, with a preferable crust-to-fruit ratio, in my humble opinion. They bake up faster than a large pie, can be taken along on car rides or picnics, and fit easily into lunch bags and backpacks. On special occasions I serve them with Crème Fraîche (page 305) or Rosemary No-Churn Ice Cream (page 295).

makes 2 hand pies

1 recipe Single-Crust Pie Dough (page 183)

1½ cups (255 g) blackberries, cut in half

1 teaspoon lemon juice

½ teaspoon pure vanilla extract

2 tablespoons sugar, plus more as needed for sweetness and for sprinkling

1 tablespoon cornstarch

Pinch salt

3 tablespoons apricot jam

Egg wash (page 14)

Line a baking sheet with parchment paper.

Lightly flour a work surface. Roll the Single-Crust Pie Dough into a 12½-inch square, flouring the dough as needed so it doesn't stick. Trim the sides of the square with a pastry cutter and discard the excess. Cut the dough into 4 equal squares. Transfer the squares to the prepared pan (they may overlap a bit) and put the baking sheet in the fridge while you prepare the filling.

Combine the blackberries, lemon juice, and vanilla in a large bowl. In a small bowl, combine the sugar, cornstarch, and salt. Add the sugar mixture to the berries and toss gently to combine. Taste the blackberries. If extra sugar is needed, add 1 to 2 tablespoons more.

Remove the pastry from the fridge and distribute the jam evenly over the surface of 2 squares. Divide the fruit evenly on top, leaving a 1-inch border around the edges (the fruit will be mounded quite a bit in the center). Top each fruit-covered square with one of the remaining pieces of pastry and press firmly around the borders with a fork to crimp the edges of the dough. Place the baking sheet in the freezer to chill.

Adjust an oven rack to the lower middle position. Preheat the oven to 400°F.

Remove the baking sheet from the freezer, cut a small X in the center of each square to vent the pastry, and then gently brush the tops with the egg wash. Sprinkle the tops generously with sugar. Bake 25 to 30 minutes, until the crusts are deep golden and the juices are bubbling. Move the pan to a wire rack and let the handpies cool on the pan before serving.

AMARETTO TARTLETS

I worked as a barista at a small café in Minneapolis where the baker made the most beautiful fruit tarts throughout the summer months. They would sell out in minutes; customers loved their creamy centers and fresh fruit toppings. One afternoon I jotted down the recipe for the amaretto filling and have carried it with me ever since. I pair it here with a sweet crust and a jam swirl, so the tartlets can also be made in the winter months when berries are not in season. *makes 6 tartlets*

SHORTBREAD CRUST

2 cups (284 g) all-purpose flour

¼ cup (50 g) sugar

½ teaspoon salt

10 tablespoons (1¼ sticks; 142 g) unsalted butter, cold and sliced into about 14 slices

1 large egg

1 large yolk

1 teaspoon pure vanilla extract

Egg wash (page 14)

AMARETTO FILLING

16 ounces (452 g) cream cheese, room temperature

½ cup (99 g) sugar

3 tablespoons Amaretto liqueur

1 teaspoon pure vanilla extract

1 teaspoon almond extract

Pinch salt

⅓ cup raspberry or other berry-flavored jam

FOR THE SHORTBREAD CRUST: In the bowl of a stand mixer fitted with a paddle, mix together the flour, sugar, and salt on low until combined. Add the butter and mix on low until the butter is incorporated and resembles coarse sand. Add the egg, egg yolk, and vanilla and mix on low until the dough comes together in a ball.

Divide the dough equally among six 4-inch tartlet pans with removable bottoms. Using your hands, press about two-thirds of the dough into the bottom of each pan, and then press the remaining dough into the fluted sides of the pan. Press and smooth dough with your hands to an even thickness. Place the tartlet pans on a sheet pan and place in the freezer, chilling the dough until firm, 20 to 30 minutes.

Adjust an oven rack to the lower middle position. Preheat the oven to 350°F. Remove the pan from the freezer. Line each tartlet pan with parchment paper, covering the edges to prevent burning. Fill the centers with pie weights.

Bake 18 to 22 minutes, until light golden brown and the dough is no longer

CONTINUED

wet. Remove the tart pan from the oven and carefully remove the pie weights and parchment. Brush the center of each tart with egg wash. Return the pan to the oven and bake 3 to 6 minutes, until deep golden brown. Transfer the pan to a wire rack and let cool completely. Finish the tart as directed in the recipe.

FOR THE FILLING: In a stand mixer fitted with a paddle, beat cream cheese on medium until smooth. Add the sugar and beat on medium until smooth. Add the amaretto, vanilla, almond, and salt and mix on low until combined. Increase to medium and beat again until light and creamy, 1 minute. Divide the mixture evenly among the cooled tartlets. Top each tartlet with 1 tablespoon jam and use a butter knife to swirl it into the filling. Chill until firm, about 30 minutes.

NOTE: I like a strong amaretto flavor here, but you can add half the amount for a lighter flavor.

BUTTERSCOTCH CRUMBLE

Technically this probably doesn't belong in a pie and tart chapter because it is essentially butterscotch pudding with a pecan-streusel topping. But it's so delicious I decided to pass it off as a crumble anyway. The pudding is sweet and salty, the streusel adds a lovely bit of crunch, and the pecans accent the butterscotch perfectly.

makes 6 mini crumbles

1 cup Streusel (page 312)

2 cups whole milk

1 cup heavy cream

½ cup (99 g) granulated sugar

½ cup (99 g) packed brown sugar

1 teaspoon salt

4 large egg yolks

¼ cup (28 g) cornstarch

8 tablespoons (1 stick; 113 g) unsalted butter, room temperature, cut into 4 pieces

1 tablespoon pure vanilla extract

1 tablespoon blackstrap rum or bourbon

½ cup (57 g) whole pecans, toasted and chopped into small pieces

Adjust an oven rack to the middle position. Preheat the oven to 350°F. Line a baking sheet with parchment paper.

Place the streusel on the baking sheet in an even layer. Bake 10 to 12 minutes, until golden brown. Cool completely.

In a small saucepan over medium heat, heat the milk and heavy cream until just simmering. Remove from the heat and transfer to a medium liquid measuring cup with a pourable spout.

In the bowl of a stand mixer fitted with a paddle, beat the granulated and brown sugars, salt, and egg yolks on low until combined. Increase to medium-high and beat until very thick, about 5 minutes. Scrape down the sides of the bowl and add the cornstarch. Mix on low until combined. With the mixer running on low, slowly pour in the hot milk mixture, beating until incorporated.

Transfer the mixture to a medium, heavy-bottomed saucepan. Cook over medium heat, stirring constantly, until the mixture becomes thick and begins to boil, 6 to 8 minutes. Whisk the mixture until it becomes the consistency of pudding and is glossy, 3 to 4 minutes. Remove from the heat and stir in the butter, vanilla, and rum. Strain the

CONTINUED

mixture through a mesh strainer into a medium bowl. Cover with plastic wrap, making sure the wrap sits directly on top of the pudding (this will help keep it from forming a skin). Place the bowl in the freezer for 15 minutes, then transfer to the refrigerator until well chilled, at least 4 hours. Divide the pudding in between six ramekins and top with the pecans and a scant layer of streusel. Pass the remaining streusel while serving; guests can add as needed.

NOTES: The streusel adds crunch, but it also adds extra sweetness; if you don't want to make the pudding any sweeter, you can just top it with the pecans.

I add only a small amount of streusel to start with; this helps it not to get soggy, and guests can add more as they prefer.

Cookies were the reason I first got into the kitchen, and while I now enjoy making more complicated pastries and desserts, I still get excited about a fresh-baked dozen. The whole cookie-making process in itself is rewarding. The dough is delicious and is able to be easily sneaked without ruining a recipe. Mixing the ingredients is not complicated, and the preparation time is short. The cookies can be eaten almost immediately upon exiting the oven, giving instant gratification to those eagerly waiting for peanut butter or oatmeal or chocolate chip.

Standouts in this chapter include Chocolate Chip Cookies (facing page), a classic that never goes out of style. I've been making Coffee Blondies (page 258) for years and they never disappoint, and Lime-Mint Bars (page 266) with Whipped Cream are a new family favorite.

CHOCOLATE CHIP COOKIES

Originally I thought to include a different chocolate chip cookie recipe in this book. It was my go-to cookie, one I had made for years at Bordertown Coffee. I began working on a thin and crispy version, and along the way it evolved into this recipe. The cookie falls somewhere in the middle of gooey and crispy, with edges that shatter in your mouth and a center that is soft and full of chocolate. My family loved it so much that my original recipe hasn't seen the light of day since. Meet our new house cookie. *makes 10 cookies*

2 cups (284 g) all-purpose flour

½ teaspoon baking soda

¾ teaspoon salt

½ pound (2 sticks; 227 g) unsalted butter, room temperature

1½ cups (297 g) granulated sugar

¼ cup (50 g) packed brown sugar

1 large egg

1½ teaspoons pure vanilla extract

2 tablespoons water

6 ounces (170 g) bittersweet chocolate, chopped into bite-size pieces averaging ½ inch with some smaller and some larger

Adjust an oven rack to the middle position. Preheat the oven to 350°F. Line 3 baking sheets with aluminum foil, dull side up.

In a small bowl, whisk the flour, baking soda, and salt.

In the bowl of a stand mixer fitted with a paddle, beat the butter on medium until creamy. Add the granulated and brown sugars and beat on medium until light and fluffy, 2 to 3 minutes. Add the egg, vanilla, and water and mix on low to combine. Add the flour mixture and mix on low until combined. Add the chocolate and mix on low into the batter.

Form the dough into 3½-ounce (100 g) balls (a heaping ⅓ cup each). Place 4 balls an equal distance apart on a prepared pan and transfer to the freezer for 15 minutes before baking. After you put the first baking sheet in the oven, put the second one in the freezer.

Place the chilled baking sheet in the oven and bake 10 minutes, until the cookies are puffed slightly in the center. Lift the side of the baking sheet up about 4 inches and gently let it drop down against the oven rack, so the edges of the cookies set and the inside falls back down (this will feel wrong, but trust me). After the cookies puff

CONTINUED

up again in 2 minutes, repeat lifting and dropping the pan. Repeat a few more times to create ridges around the edge of the cookie. Bake 16 to 18 minutes total, until the cookies have spread out and the edges are golden brown but the centers are much lighter and not fully cooked.

Transfer the baking sheet to a wire rack; let cool completely before removing the cookies from the pan.

VARIATION

chocolate chip cookies with toasted sesame oil · Add 2 tablespoons of toasted sesame oil along with the vanilla. Toasted sesame oil may sound like an odd addition, but it lends a delicious depth of flavor and pairs wonderfully with the sugar and chocolate.

NOTES: These cookies are rather large, but to get the edges to spread out and crinkle, they need to be on the big side. If you want to make the cookies smaller, you won't get as many ridges on the outer layer, and your center won't be quite as gooey. They will still be delicious, but not quite what I intended for you.

If you skip freezing the cookies, they will spread too much on the pan and will not form the crinkly outer layer.

Chocolate chips are not a good substitution for the chopped chocolate; the cookies will not turn out the same with chips. If you do still want to use chocolate chips, you will need to use 8 ounces chips and make the cookies 2½ ounces big.

Using the dull side of aluminum foil to bake these cookies is a little trick I learned after hearing Alice Medrich speak. The foil helps make for an extra-crisp, golden brown bottom. Parchment paper can also be used with good results.

The cookies are delicious warm, but I've found I love them a couple of days later just as much. I usually store them in the fridge and sneak pieces of them cold.

PEANUT BUTTER COOKIES

I'm going to admit it: I love eating cookie dough just as much as I like eating the actual cookie itself, and this dough just might be my favorite. Peanut butter cookies are a household classic; salty and sweet, sprinkled with sugar, and delicious eaten warm or cold. I stray from the traditional method of flattening the cookie and adding a crisscross shape; instead the cookies are rolled in sugar and baked in ball form.

makes 12 to 14 cookies

1½ cups (213 g) all-purpose flour

1 teaspoon baking soda

1 teaspoon salt

½ pound (2 sticks; 227 g) unsalted butter, room temperature

½ cup (99 g) granulated sugar, plus 1 cup (198 g) for rolling

½ cup (99 g) packed brown sugar

1 cup creamy peanut butter

1 large egg

2 teaspoons pure vanilla extract

Adjust the oven rack to the middle position. Preheat oven to 350°F. Line two baking sheets with parchment paper.

In a medium bowl, whisk the flour, baking soda, and salt.

In the bowl of a stand mixer fitted with a paddle, beat the butter on medium until smooth. Add the ½ cup granulated sugar and the brown sugar and beat on medium until light and fluffy, 2 to 3 minutes. Add the peanut butter and beat on medium until fully combined. Add the egg and vanilla and beat on medium until smooth. Add the flour mixture and beat on low until just combined.

Put the remaining 1 cup sugar into a small bowl.

Form the dough into 3-ounce (85g) balls (a scant ⅓ cup each), rolling each one in the bowl of sugar to coat before placing it on the baking sheet. Put 6 or 7 cookies on each sheet.

Bake one sheet at a time 10 to 12 minutes, rotating the pan halfway through, until the cookies have spread and the edges are set.

Transfer the pan to a wire rack and let the cookies cool completely on the pan.

VARIATION

extra peanut butter cookies · Use crunchy peanut butter in place of the creamy, and add 1 cup (170 g) peanut butter chips to the dough after the flour mixture is added.

OATMEAL COOKIES
WITH WHITE CHOCOLATE AND GOLDEN RAISINS

One Friday night, after closing down the Blue Heron, I stayed after hours to make twelve dozen oatmeal raisin cookies that needed to be picked up the next morning at 7:00. Our oven space was limited, and we could bake only one tray at a time, so I worked in the kitchen until 2:00 A.M.: mixing dough, shaping circles, filling sheet pans, and then waiting for cookies to cool so I could package them all up. I fell in love with oatmeal raisin cookies that night; after nibbling on too much dough and the random wonky-shaped cookie, I grew to appreciate their chewy, raisin-filled texture by the light of the moon. Chocolate chip cookies may always be at the top of my list, but these round raisin treats run a very close second. This version includes white chocolate, a dash of nutmeg, and the fancier golden raisin for an upscale cookie that is nothing short of delicious. *makes 12 to 14 cookies*

1 cup (142 g) all-purpose flour

¾ teaspoon baking soda

½ teaspoon salt

¼ teaspoon grated nutmeg

12 tablespoons (1½ sticks; 170 g) unsalted butter, room temperature

⅓ cup (66 g) granulated sugar

¾ cup (149 g) packed brown sugar

1 large egg

2 teaspoons pure vanilla extract

2¼ cups (203 g) rolled oats

5 ounces (142 g) white chocolate, chopped

¾ cup (110 g) golden raisins

Adjust an oven rack to the middle position. Preheat the oven to 350°F. Line two baking sheets with parchment paper.

In a medium bowl, whisk the flour, baking soda, salt, and nutmeg.

In the bowl of a stand mixer fitted with a paddle, beat the butter on medium until smooth. Add the granulated and brown sugars and beat on medium until light and fluffy, 2 to 3 minutes. Add the egg and vanilla and mix on medium until combined. Add the flour mixture and mix on low until just combined. Add the oats, chocolate, and raisins and mix on low until combined. Using a spatula, stir the batter to incorporate any stray oats on the bottom of the mixing bowl.

Form the dough into 3-ounce (85 g) balls (a scant ⅓ cup each) and put 6 or 7 on a baking sheet.

Bake one sheet at a time 10 to 12 minutes, until the sides are golden brown and the tops are just starting to brown but are still underdone (the very center will still be pale).

Transfer the baking sheet to a wire rack and let cool 5 minutes. Remove the cookies from the pan and let cool completely on a wire rack.

VARIATION

oatmeal cookies with fleur de sel · Sprinkle fleur de sel (just a pinch or two) on each cookie right after they come out of the oven.

GRANOLA CHOCOLATE PECAN COOKIES

One afternoon as I set out to bake oatmeal raisin cookies, I realized too late that I was out of not only raisins but oats as well. There was a tray of maple-cinnamon granola cooling on my counter and, making a quick decision, I replaced the oats with it, along with chocolate for the raisins. It was a lucky swap, and the cookies have become a favorite in our home. The granola and pecans give the cookie a nice bit of crunch, and the chocolate and cinnamon complement each other in every bite. *makes 12 to 14 cookies*

2¼ cups (225 g) Maple-Cinnamon Granola (page 36)

1 cup (142 g) all-purpose flour

¾ teaspoon baking soda

½ teaspoon salt

12 tablespoons (1½ sticks; 170 g) unsalted butter, room temperature

⅓ cup (66 g) granulated sugar

¾ cup (149 g) packed brown sugar

1 large egg

2 teaspoons pure vanilla extract

5 ounces (143 g) bittersweet chocolate, chopped

¾ cup (86 g) pecan halves, toasted and chopped

Adjust an oven rack to the middle position. Preheat the oven to 350°F. Line two baking sheets with parchment paper.

In a medium bowl, whisk the flour, baking soda, and salt.

In the bowl of a stand mixer fitted with a paddle, beat the butter on medium until smooth. Add the granulated and brown sugars and beat on medium until light and fluffy, 2 to 3 minutes. Add the egg and vanilla and mix on medium until combined. Add the flour mixture and mix on low until just combined. Add the granola, chocolate, and pecans and mix on low to combine. Using a spatula, stir the batter to incorporate any stray granola on the bottom of the mixing bowl.

Form the dough into 3-ounce (85 g) balls (about ¼ cup each) and put 6 or 7 on a baking sheet.

Bake one sheet at a time 12 to 15 minutes, until the sides are golden brown and the top is just starting to brown but the very center is still slightly underdone. Transfer the baking sheet to a wire rack and let cool 5 minutes. Remove the cookies from the pan and let cool completely on a wire rack.

CHOCOLATE SUGAR COOKIES

I often find myself craving a piece of chocolate in the afternoons, as it goes rather nicely with the cup of hot coffee that is also a necessity in my daily life. Most days a little square of bittersweet will do, but other times something more extravagant is essential. I have found these chocolate sugar cookies do the trick; they are soft and delicious without being overly rich and sweet. *makes 11 to 12 large cookies*

1¾ cups (249 g) all-purpose flour

½ cup (50 g) natural cocoa powder, or a combination cocoa powder

¾ teaspoon baking soda

½ teaspoon salt

1 cup (227 g) unsalted butter, room temperature

1¾ cups (347 g) sugar, plus 1 cup (198 g) for rolling

1 large egg

1 teaspoon pure vanilla extract

Adjust an oven rack to the middle position. Preheat the oven to 350°F. Line two baking sheets with parchment paper.

In a medium bowl, combine the flour, cocoa powder, baking soda, and salt.

In the bowl of a stand mixer fitted with a paddle, beat the butter on medium until smooth. Add the 1¾ cups sugar and beat on medium until light and fluffy, 2 to 3 minutes. Add the egg and vanilla and beat on medium until combined. Add the flour mixture and beat on low until just combined.

Place the remaining 1 cup of the sugar in a medium bowl.

Form the cookies into 3-ounce (85 g) balls (a scant ⅓ cup each). Roll each ball in the sugar and place 6 cookies on each prepared sheet pan. Bake one sheet at a time 11 to 14 minutes, until the edges have set and the centers are puffed and starting to crackle.

Transfer the baking sheet to a wire rack and let the cookies cool completely on the pan.

VARIATION

chocolate-cardamom cookies · Add 1 teaspoon ground cardamom to the sugar used for rolling.

OLIVE OIL SUGAR COOKIES
WITH PISTACHIOS AND LEMON GLAZE

My mom will often turn down the sweet, gooey confections that I prefer, but she can never say no to a thin, crispy cookie. I created these unique cookies with her in mind.

Olive oil is becoming a more common ingredient in baking, and it pairs well with pistachios and lemon in this recipe. The olive oil flavor here is subtle, but there is still a trace of fruitiness and spice, and the sweet lemon glaze is a nice partner. *makes 24 cookies*

⅓ cup (43 g) shelled pistachios, plus ⅓ cup (43 g) chopped for sprinkling

2 cups (284 g) all-purpose flour

½ teaspoon baking soda

½ teaspoon salt

4 tablespoons (57 g) unsalted butter, room temperature

¾ cup (149 g) granulated sugar

¼ cup (29 g) confectioners' sugar

½ cup olive oil

1 large egg

1 teaspoon pure vanilla extract

LEMON GLAZE

1 cup (113 g) confectioners' sugar

Grated zest of 1 lemon

1 tablespoon lemon juice

2 to 4 tablespoons heavy cream or milk

FOR THE COOKIES: Adjust the oven rack to the middle position. Preheat the oven to 350°F. Line two baking sheets with parchment paper.

Place the pistachios in a food processor fitted with a steel blade and pulse until finely ground. Add the flour, baking soda, and salt. Pulse to fully combine and set aside.

In the bowl of a stand mixer fitted with a paddle, beat the butter on medium until creamy. Add the granulated and confectioners' sugars and beat on medium until light and fluffy, 2 to 3 minutes. Add the olive oil and mix on low until combined. Scrape down the sides of the bowl and add the egg and vanilla, mixing on low until combined. Add the flour mixture and mix on low until combined.

Gather the dough, wrap with plastic wrap, and chill in the refrigerator for at least 2 hours and up to 1 day.

Lightly flour a work surface and roll the dough to ¼ inch thick. Using a 2-inch biscuit or cookie cutter, cut out circles. (Any dough scraps can be rewrapped and chilled while the cookies are baking.) Gently slide a metal spatula underneath each round and transfer it to the prepared baking sheet. Place 12 cookies on each sheet. Put the first baking sheet in the freezer for 10 minutes. After the dough has chilled, put the first pan of cookies in the oven, and then put the second pan in the freezer. Repeat with the leftover dough.

Bake one sheet at a time, 10 to 12 minutes, until the cookies are just beginning to brown on the edges.

Transfer the baking sheet to a wire rack and let the cookies cool completely on the pan.

FOR THE LEMON GLAZE: In a small bowl, whisk the confectioners' sugar and lemon zest. Whisk in the lemon juice. Whisk in the heavy cream, 1 tablespoon at a time. Add just enough cream to make a thin glaze. Using an offset spatula or kitchen knife, spread a thin layer of the glaze on each cooled cookie. Sprinkle with the chopped pistachios and let the glaze set a few minutes before serving.

SPICE COOKIES WITH COFFEE GLAZE

I've never been a huge fan of molasses cookies, but I often crave a cookie jam-packed with spices. This version bakes up perfectly crisp, and the coffee glaze pairs well with the cinnamon, cardamom, ginger, and pepper. *makes 24 cookies*

2¼ cups (320 g) all-purpose flour

½ teaspoon baking soda

½ teaspoon salt

¾ teaspoon ground cinnamon

½ teaspoon ground ginger

½ teaspoon ground cardamom

Pinch black pepper

12 tablespoons (1½ sticks; 170 g) unsalted butter

1 cup (198 g) granulated sugar

¼ cup (50 g) packed brown sugar

1 large egg

1 teaspoon pure vanilla extract

COFFEE GLAZE

1 cup (114 g) confectioners' sugar

2 tablespoons strong coffee, cold

½ teaspoon pure vanilla extract

2 to 4 tablespoons heavy cream or milk

Adjust an oven rack to the middle position. Preheat the oven to 350°F. Line two baking sheets with parchment paper.

In a medium bowl, whisk the flour, baking soda, salt, cinnamon, ginger, cardamom, and pepper.

In the bowl of a stand mixer fitted with a paddle, beat the butter on medium until smooth. Add the granulated and brown sugars and beat on medium until light and fluffy, 2 to 3 minutes. Add the egg and vanilla and mix on medium until combined. Add the flour mixture and mix on low until just combined.

Gather the dough, flatten into a disc, and wrap with plastic wrap. Chill for at least 2 hours and up to 1 day.

Lightly flour a work surface and roll the dough to ¼ inch thick. Using a 2-inch biscuit or cookie cutter, cut out circles. (Any dough scraps can be rewrapped and chilled while the cookies are baking.) Gently slide a metal spatula underneath each round and transfer it to a prepared baking sheet. Place 12 on each sheet. Put the first baking sheet in the freezer for 10 minutes. After the dough has chilled, put the first pan of cookies in the oven, and then put the second pan in the freezer. Repeat with the leftover dough.

CONTINUED

Bake one sheet at a time 10 to 12 minutes, until the cookies are just beginning to brown on the edges. Transfer the baking sheet to a wire rack and let the cookies cool completely on the pan.

FOR THE GLAZE: In a small bowl, whisk the confectioners' sugar, coffee, and vanilla. Whisk in the heavy cream 1 tablespoon at a time. Add just enough cream to make a thin glaze. Using an offset spatula or kitchen knife, spread a thin layer of the glaze on each cooled cookie. Let the glaze set a few minutes before serving.

SHORTBREAD WITH CHOCOLATE

This crisp, buttery cookie is easy to make, and goes with everything. Dunked in coffee, coated in a confectioners' sugar glaze, or standing alone, shortbread is downright delicious. I found a slight drizzle of chocolate just might make this cookie absolutely perfect, and I took some pleasure in treating the pan of cookies like an abstract painting. *makes 30 to 35 cookies*

1 cup (142 g) all-purpose flour

⅓ cup (38 g) confectioners' sugar

½ teaspoon salt

1 vanilla bean, seeds scraped

8 tablespoons (1 stick; 113 g) unsalted butter, room temperature, cut into 1-inch pieces

CHOCOLATE TOPPING

2 ounces (57 g) bittersweet chocolate, chopped into small pieces

Adjust an oven rack to the middle position. Preheat the oven to 350°F. Line two baking sheets with parchment paper.

In the bowl of a stand mixer fitted with a paddle, combine the flour, confectioners' sugar, salt, and vanilla bean seeds on low speed. Add the butter one piece at a time and mix on medium until it is incorporated and the dough starts to form a ball. Dump the dough out onto a lightly floured work surface, shape into a flat disc, and wrap in plastic. Refrigerate 30 minutes.

Lightly flour a work surface and roll the dough into a large, ½-inch-thick square. Using a 2-inch biscuit or cookie cutter, cut out circles. (Any dough scraps can be rewrapped and chilled while the cookies are baking.) Gently slide a metal spatula underneath each round and transfer it to a prepared baking sheet. Place 12 on each sheet.

Bake one sheet at a time, 15 to 17 minutes, until the edges begin to brown.

Transfer the pan to a wire rack and allow the cookies to cool completely before drizzling with chocolate.

FOR THE CHOCOLATE: Put about 1 inch of water in a medium saucepan and bring it to a gentle boil.

CONTINUED

Melt 1 ounce of the chocolate in a heatproof bowl set over the pan of boiling water, being careful not to let the water touch the bottom of the bowl. Stir constantly until just melted. Add the remaining 1 ounce and stir until the chocolate is completely smooth. Set aside to cool to room temperature.

TO DECORATE: Keep the cookies on the baking sheet. Spoon the room-temperature chocolate into a zipper-lock bag and close to seal, then snip the tip to make a very small opening. If the opening is too big, the chocolate will flow out too fast. Drizzle the chocolate back and forth over the cookies, making criss-cross patterns (or any other pattern you like). Let the chocolate set before removing the cookies from the pan (unless, of course, you need to eat one right away).

BROWNIES

When you first bite into these chocolate pieces, the deep, dark cocoa flavor will hit. You will shut your eyes as words like *dreamy, impeccable,* and *sexy* flood your mind. A minute later you will pick up the knife and cut off another square, and feel no guilt for indulging again. ***makes 12 large or 24 small bars***

8 tablespoons (1 stick; 113 g) unsalted butter, cold

8 ounces (226 g) bittersweet chocolate, chopped

¼ cup (25 g) Dutch process cocoa powder

1 cup plus 2 tablespoons (160 g) all-purpose flour

½ teaspoon baking powder

¾ teaspoon salt

4 large eggs

½ cup canola oil

1½ cups (297 g) granulated sugar

½ cup (99 g) packed brown sugar

2 teaspoons pure vanilla extract

Adjust an oven rack to the lower middle position. Preheat the oven to 350°F. Grease a 9 by 13-inch baking pan and line a parchment sling (page 15).

In a medium saucepan over medium-low heat, melt the butter and the bittersweet chocolate until both are melted and smooth. Remove from the heat and add the cocoa powder, stirring until smooth. Set aside to cool slightly.

In a small bowl, whisk the flour, baking powder, and salt.

In a large bowl, whisk the eggs, oil, sugars, and vanilla. Add the slightly cooled chocolate mixture and whisk until smooth. Add the flour mixture and stir with a spatula until just combined. Pour the batter into the prepared pan and bake 22 to 27 minutes, until the sides of the brownies have set, the top is beginning to crackle and look glossy, and a wooden skewer or toothpick inserted into the center comes out with crumbs. The batter on the skewer should not be wet, but should have a good amount of crumbs clinging to it.

Transfer the pan to a wire rack and let cool completely. Use the parchment paper sling to gently lift the brownies from the pan. Cut them into squares.

VARIATION

peanut butter brownies · Take ¾ cup of creamy peanut butter and drop it in circles over the brownie batter before baking. Using an offset spatula or butter knife, drag the peanut butter through the top of the batter, making swirls. Bake as directed.

COFFEE BLONDIES

There are times when comfort and familiarity are so important, where vices are needed to just get us through, to keep us connected to *something* in difficult times. This recipe is one that gives me solace and grounds my soul. It started as a newspaper clipping that made its way into the Blue Heron kitchen, and I have continued to make it for almost two decades. It's peeked out of every bake case I have stocked, graced my kitchen table at birthday parties and baby dedications, brought me relief after a long day, and soothed tears at funeral luncheons. The combination of coffee and chocolate makes for blondies that are both unique and indulgent. I hope you find some comfort in them, too. *makes 12 large or 24 small blondies*

1½ cups (213 g) all-purpose flour

1½ teaspoons baking powder

12 tablespoons (1½ sticks; 170 g) unsalted butter, cold

1½ cups (297 g) packed brown sugar

¾ teaspoon salt

2 tablespoons strong coffee, room temperature

1 egg

1½ tablespoons pure vanilla extract

¾ cup (86 g) pecan halves, toasted and chopped

¾ cup (128 g) bittersweet or semisweet chocolate chips

Adjust the oven rack to the middle position. Preheat the oven to 350°F. Grease a 9 by 13-inch baking pan and line it with a parchment sling (page 15).

In a medium bowl, whisk the flour and baking powder.

In a medium saucepan over medium heat, melt the butter, brown sugar, and salt. Remove from the heat and stir in the coffee until well combined. Let the mixture cool to room temperature. Add the egg and vanilla and whisk until combined. Transfer the mixture to a large bowl. Add the flour mixture and stir until just combined. Add the pecans and chocolate chips and stir gently.

Spread the batter evenly into the prepared pan and bake 18 to 24 minutes, until the blondies are set on the edges and the top is golden brown and just beginning to form cracks. A wooden skewer or toothpick inserted into the blondies should come out with just a couple of crumbs.

Transfer the pan to a wire rack and let cool completely. Use the parchment sling to gently lift the blondies from the pan. Cut them into squares.

MINT CHOCOLATE BARS

The grasshopper is a famous flavor combination that appears in both drink and pie forms, and for good reason; mint and chocolate are never a bad pair. I took my brownie recipe, added a generous layer of mint buttercream, and then topped things off with a silky smooth layer of chocolate ganache. I find a small square is the perfect way to enjoy these, although it is almost impossible to eat just one. ***makes 12 large or 24 small bars***

1 recipe Brownies (page 257), cooled completely and refrigerated in the pan for 30 minutes

MINT BUTTERCREAM

1 cup (227 g) unsalted butter, room temperature

2 tablespoons crème de menthe

1 teaspoon pure vanilla extract

½ teaspoon mint extract

Pinch salt

2 cups (226 g) confectioners' sugar

1 recipe Chocolate Ganache (page 309), cooled to room temperature

FOR THE MINT BUTTERCREAM: In the bowl of a stand mixer fitted with a paddle, beat the butter on medium until smooth. Add the crème de menthe, vanilla, mint extract, and salt and beat on medium to combine. Turn the mixer to low and slowly add the confectioners' sugar, mixing until combined. Scrape down the sides of the bowl and beat on medium-high until fluffy and light, 5 to 7 minutes.

TO ASSEMBLE AND SERVE: Spread the mint filling evenly on top of the chilled brownies. Return the pan to the fridge and chill for 1 hour. Pour the cooled ganache over the top of the chilled buttercream and, using an offset spatula, spread it in an even layer. Return the pan to the fridge for 1 hour.

Remove the pan from the fridge and let sit 10 minutes before cutting, to allow the glaze to soften slightly. Cut into squares and serve.

NOTE: If you don't particularly care for the crispy edges on your brownies, slice them off before frosting and coating the bars.

BLUEBERRY-APPLE CRUMBLE BARS

Minnesota is known for its potluck culture, and I've made plenty of bars over the years to share at get-togethers, church picnics, and funerals. These are my go-to bars on most occasions; the shortbread crust, blueberry-apple filling, and streusel top are always a hit. This recipe can be doubled and baked in a half sheet pan, making it perfect for larger gatherings. *makes 12 large or 24 small bars*

CRUST

2½ cups (355 g) all-purpose flour

½ cup (45 g) rolled or quick oats

1 cup (198 g) sugar

1 teaspoon baking powder

½ teaspoon salt

½ teaspoon cinnamon

½ pound (2 sticks; 227 g) unsalted butter, at room temperature, and sliced into 1-inch pieces

BLUEBERRY FILLING

5 heaping cups blueberries (700 g)

½ cup (75 g) grated Gala apple (about one small apple)

1 tablespoon lemon juice

⅓ cup (66 g) sugar

2 tablespoons cornstarch

Pinch salt

Adjust an oven rack to the middle position. Preheat the oven to 350°F. Grease a 9 by 13-inch baking pan and line it with a parchment sling (see page 15).

In the bowl of a stand mixer fitted with a paddle, mix the flour, oats, sugars, baking soda, salt, and cinnamon on low to combine. Add the butter and mix on medium until mixture resembles coarse sand.

Press half the flour-oat mixture into the bottom of the prepared pan. Bake 10 minutes. Prepare the berry filling while the crust is baking (see below). Remove the pan from the oven, spread the berry mixture over the crust, and sprinkle the remaining crumble mixture evenly over the top. Bake 20 to 25 minutes, until the crumbly top is light golden brown.

Transfer to a wire rack and let cool. Place the pan in the fridge and let chill 4 to 6 hours. Slice bars and serve. The bars can be served cold or at room temperature, but keep best in the fridge.

FOR THE BERRY FILLING: In a large bowl, mix the berries, apple, and lemon juice.

In a small bowl, combine the sugar, cornstarch, cinnamon, and salt. Pour the sugar mixture over the berries and stir gently with a spatula to evenly combine.

CHOCOLATE OAT BARS

One evening, when I was supposed to be making lemon oat bars for a family get-together, I decided I was actually in the mood for chocolate and changed my mind halfway through mixing the crust. I never regretted that decision. These bars are similar to old-school oatmeal fudge bars, except the filling here contains sweetened condensed milk, which makes for a smooth, rich center. They are creamy and delicious, with a firm base that gives just enough crunch to complement the filling. *makes 12 large or 24 small bars*

Two 14-ounce cans (792 g) sweetened condensed milk

7 ounces (198 g) bittersweet chocolate, melted

2 tablespoons heavy cream

2 teaspoons pure vanilla extract

½ teaspoon salt

2 cups (284 g) all-purpose flour

1½ cups (135 g) rolled or quick oats

¼ cup (50 g) granulated sugar

½ cup (99 g) packed brown sugar

½ teaspoon baking soda

½ teaspoon salt

½ pound (2 sticks; 227 g) unsalted butter, room temperature, and sliced into ½-inch pieces

Adjust an oven rack to the middle position. Preheat the oven to 350°F. Grease a 9 by 13-inch pan and line it with a parchment sling (page 15).

In a large bowl, whisk the sweetened condensed milk, chocolate, heavy cream, vanilla, and salt until smooth.

In the bowl of a stand mixer fitted with a paddle, mix the flour, oats, granulated and brown sugars, baking soda, and salt on low to combine. Add the butter and mix on medium until the mixture is crumbly.

Press half of the oat mixture into the bottom of the prepared pan. Bake 10 minutes. Remove the pan from the oven and carefully spread the chocolate mixture over the crust. Sprinkle the remaining oat mixture evenly over the top. Bake 15 to 20 minutes, until the chocolate has puffed up a bit and does not jiggle, and the crumbly top is light golden brown.

Transfer the pan to a wire rack and let cool. Place the pan in the fridge and chill for 4 to 6 hours. Slice the bars and serve. The bars can be served cold or at room temperature, but keep best in the fridge.

LIME-MINT BARS

My dad loves my Key lime pie. He asks for it every year on his birthday, a request I am happy to fill. After years of making traditional pies, I realized the same flavors work quite nicely in bar form. Now my dad (and the rest of us) can have bite-size squares of this favorite dessert more often. Mint whipped cream here may seem unusual, but lime and mint see eye to eye. *makes 9 bars*

CRUST

1½ cups (150 g) graham cracker crumbs (or 11 whole graham crackers pulsed in a food processor)

3 tablespoons sugar

5 tablespoons (65 g) unsalted butter, melted and cooled

FILLING

4 large egg yolks

½ cup lime juice

2 tablespoons heavy cream

1 teaspoon pure vanilla extract

1 tablespoon grated lime zest

¼ teaspoon salt

One 14-ounce can (396 g) sweetened condensed milk

1 to 2 drops green food coloring (optional)

WHIPPED CREAM

4 ounces (113 g) cream cheese, room temperature

2 tablespoons sugar

2 tablespoons crème de menthe

½ teaspoon mint extract

½ teaspoon pure vanilla extract

Pinch salt

1½ cups heavy cream

FOR THE CRUST: Adjust an oven rack to the lower middle position. Preheat the oven to 325°F. Grease an 8-inch-square baking pan and line with a parchment sling (page 15).

In a medium bowl, mix the graham cracker crumbs and sugar. Add the butter to the crumbs and stir until all the crumbs are coated. Use a measuring cup or spoon to press the crumbs evenly onto the bottom of the prepared pan.

Bake 12 to 15 minutes, until lightly browned and fragrant. Transfer the pan to a wire rack and let cool slightly.

FOR THE FILLING: In a large bowl, whisk the egg yolks, lime juice, heavy cream, vanilla, lime zest, salt, and sweetened condensed milk until smooth and fully combined. Add

CONTINUED

the food coloring (if desired) and stir to evenly distribute. Pour the filling onto the warm crust. Bake 14 to 17 minutes, until the center is set but still a bit wiggly when jiggled.

Transfer the pan to a wire rack and let cool completely. Place the pan in the refrigerator and chill at least 4 hours or overnight. Top the chilled bars with the mint whipped cream, slice, and serve.

FOR THE WHIPPED CREAM: In the bowl of a stand mixer fitted with a paddle, beat the cream cheese on medium until smooth. Add the sugar, crème de menthe, mint extract, vanilla, and salt. Beat on low until combined. Increase to medium and beat until smooth. Scrape down the sides of the bowl and switch to the whisk. With the mixer on low, slowly add the heavy cream, whisking until fully combined. Increase the speed to medium and beat until stiff peaks form, stopping to scrape down the sides of the bowl as needed, 2 to 3 minutes.

NOTE: The lime zest and juice will lightly color the bars green, but if you want a brighter color, you can add a drop or two of green food coloring.

MERINGUES

Meringues enchant me, bringing to my mind trees covered in new snow, and the freshly fallen flakes glistening in the early morning sun. I must admit I was never a fan of meringues until I made them myself, with a bit less sugar than normally called for. I found myself falling for them in all forms, eager to see the beautiful circles glimmering on parchment-lined trays. Here I've filled them with chocolate ganache, giving each pillow a rich, creamy center. *makes 36 meringues*

5 large egg whites

1 cup (198 g) sugar

¼ teaspoon salt

½ teaspoon pure vanilla extract

1 vanilla bean, seeds scraped

FILLING

½ cup Chocolate Ganache (page 309)

2 cups heavy whipping cream

½ teaspoon pure vanilla extract

Adjust the oven racks to the upper and lower middle positions. Preheat the oven to 200°F. Line two baking sheets with parchment paper.

Put about 1 inch of water in a medium saucepan and bring it to a gentle boil.

In the bowl of a stand mixer, stir the egg whites, sugar, and salt to combine. Place the bowl over the saucepan, being careful not to let the water touch the bottom of the bowl. Stir with a rubber spatula until the sugar is completely melted and reaches a temperature of 160°F, 4 to 5 minutes. While you are stirring, be sure to scrape down the sides of the bowl with the spatula—this will ensure no sugar grains are lurking on the sides and will help prevent the egg whites from cooking.

Remove the bowl from the heat and place it in the stand mixer fitted with a whisk. Whisk on medium-high until stiff, glossy peaks form, 8 to 10 minutes. The bowl should have cooled down to room temperature at this point. Add the vanilla and vanilla bean seeds and beat on medium-low until incorporated.

Use a spoon to mound the mixture onto the trays, making 18 meringues on each tray. Wet a spoon, and use the back to create a well in the middle of each meringue (you want the edges higher than the center to leave space for the filling). Bake the meringues for 1 hour (if you decide to bake smaller meringues, you will need to bake them for less time).

CONTINUED

Turn off the heat and allow the meringues to sit in the oven for 30 minutes. Transfer the baking sheets to wire racks and let cool completely before filling. (You can make the meringues up to 2 days in advance. Keep them in an airtight container until ready to fill.)

FOR THE FILLING: In the bowl of a stand mixer fitted with the whisk, whip the heavy cream and vanilla until soft peaks form. Stir in the chocolate ganache slightly, leaving large streaks of it in the whipped cream. Scoop the whipped cream into the wells of the meringue and serve.

VARIATIONS

meringues filled with jam · Use ½ cup of your favorite jam in place of the chocolate ganache in the filling.

cacao nib meringues with chocolate ganache · Add ½ cup cacao nibs to the meringues, along with the vanilla extract and scraped seeds.

chapter six

NO-CHURN ICE CREAM

No-churn ice cream has been around for years, with recipes and variations all over the place, in vintage cookbooks and modern magazines alike. The ice cream is smooth and rich, and while the texture is a little different from regular ice cream, it is an easy way to make a simple frozen dessert if you don't have an ice cream maker. I find myself using it quite frequently when entertaining guests, and it pairs well with so many desserts that I decided it deserved a chapter to itself here. The method is simple: Fold whipped cream into sweetened condensed milk and freeze until firm. You can get by with using only those two ingredients; however, I like to add a few others. Some salt helps cut the sweet taste. A little bit of cream cheese adds some tang which balances out the sweetness and keeps the ice cream smooth when it's frozen. Of course, adding different flavors also jazzes things up, and you'll find recipes for vanilla, chocolate, olive oil, blood orange, pumpkin, and even rosemary in this chapter.

VANILLA NO-CHURN ICE CREAM

Vanilla ice cream is a classic, with a flavor that is comforting, basic, and pleasing to almost everyone. Simple at the core, this frozen goodness goes with everything, from chocolate cake and warm brownies to peach pie and rhubarb crisp. Adding vanilla bean seeds to the base gives this freezer staple an elegant spin.

One 14-ounce can (396 g) sweetened condensed milk

1 tablespoon pure vanilla extract

1 vanilla bean, seeds scraped (optional)

¼ teaspoon salt

2 ounces (57 g) cream cheese, room temperature

2 cups heavy cream

In a large bowl, whisk the sweetened condensed milk, vanilla, vanilla bean seeds, and salt until completely combined.

In the bowl of a stand mixer fitted with a whisk, beat the cream cheese on medium until smooth. Turn the mixer to low and add the heavy cream in a slow steady stream, mixing until combined. Increase the speed to medium-high and whisk until stiff peaks form, 3 to 4 minutes.

Add half of the whipped cream mixture to the sweetened condensed milk mixture and whisk until completely combined. Using a rubber spatula, gently fold in the remaining whipped cream mixture until no streaks remain. Pour into a 9-inch loaf pan or Pullman pan with a lid and freeze until firm, 6 hours or, covered, up to 1 week.)

CHOCOLATE NO-CHURN ICE CREAM

Chocolate is a classic ice cream flavor, although richer than its vanilla counterpart. This ice cream is very decadent, and a small amount is all you need to enjoy deep chocolate flavor. It is studded with extra chocolate, and I recommend a sprinkling of fleur de sel over the top if you are a fan of the sweet and salty combination.

8 ounces (226 g) bittersweet chocolate

One 14-ounce can (396 g) sweetened condensed milk

1 teaspoon pure vanilla extract

¼ teaspoon salt

2 ounces (57 g) cream cheese, room temperature

2 cups heavy cream

Line a baking sheet with parchment paper.

Melt the chocolate in a heatproof bowl set over a pan of boiling water, being careful not to let the water touch the bottom of the bowl, and stir constantly until just melted. Remove from the heat and pour 5 ounces (a little more than half) of the chocolate onto the prepared pan. Freeze until firm, 10 to 15 minutes. Let the other 3 ounces of chocolate cool to room temperature.

In a large bowl, whisk the sweetened condensed milk, the remaining 3 ounces of cooled chocolate, vanilla, and salt until completely combined.

In the bowl of a stand mixer fitted with a whisk, beat the cream cheese on medium until smooth. Turn the mixer to low and add the heavy cream in a slow steady stream, mixing until combined. Increase the speed to medium-high and whisk until stiff peaks form, 3 to 4 minutes.

Add half the whipped cream mixture to the sweetened condensed milk mixture and whisk until completely combined. With a rubber spatula, gently fold in the remaining whipped cream mixture until no streaks remain.

Remove the chocolate from the freezer and chop it into bite-size pieces. The chocolate will begin to melt as you touch it, so work quickly. Add the chopped chocolate to the ice cream and mix to combine. Pour into a 9-inch loaf pan or Pullman pan with a lid and freeze until firm, 6 hours or, covered, up to 1 week.

NOTE: Melting the chocolate and then freezing it keeps the chocolate cold when frozen but lets it melt smooth and soft in your mouth when eating it. It's worth the extra step.

RASPBERRY NO-CHURN ICE CREAM
WITH CHOCOLATE

The summer we moved into our house, my sister and her husband gave us two raspberry bushes. We had no idea how to take care of raspberries, but we found a little home for them along our fence, dreaming of jam, and pie, and afternoon snacks. Now, years later, they are out of control—bushes racing up and down that chain link as if they own the place. We adore them, despite their wild tendencies, and every August, as the season starts slipping away a bit too soon, I am comforted by the deep pinks and reds peeking out at every turn. Raspberry ice cream has become a yearly tradition, and the kids and I spend an afternoon picking piles of berries to use. We cook them down and gently press out all their seeds, stirring the bright juice into cold cream, along with pieces of bittersweet chocolate. This is my favorite no-churn recipe in the book, one that calls to mind lazy summer days and little hands next to mine.

RASPBERRIES

4 cups (600 g) raspberries, fresh or frozen

2 tablespoons sugar

¼ teaspoon salt

CHOCOLATE PIECES

5 ounces (141 g) bittersweet chocolate

ICE CREAM

One 14-ounce can (396 g) sweetened condensed milk

1 teaspoon pure vanilla extract

¼ teaspoon salt

2 ounces (57 g) cream cheese, room temperature

2 cups heavy cream

FOR THE RASPBERRIES: Bring the raspberries, sugar, and salt to a simmer in a medium saucepan over medium-high heat. Cook, stirring and pressing down on the berries occasionally until they have released their juices, about 5 minutes. Strain the berry mixture through a fine-mesh strainer, pressing on the solids to extract as much juice as possible. Discard the solids. Let the juice cool to room temperature, then place in the refrigerator to chill.

FOR THE CHOCOLATE PIECES: Line a baking sheet with parchment paper.
    Melt the chocolate in a heatproof bowl set over a pan of boiling water, being careful not to let the water touch the bottom of the bowl. Stir constantly until just

melted. Remove from the heat and pour the mixture in the prepared pan and freeze until firm, 10 to 15 minutes. Prepare the ice cream while the chocolate is setting. When the chocolate is firm, chop it into bite-size pieces, and add to the ice cream immediately (it will start to melt as you chop it, so work quickly).

FOR THE ICE CREAM: In a large bowl, whisk the sweetened condensed milk, vanilla, salt, and chilled raspberry juice until completely combined.

In the bowl of a stand mixer fitted with a whisk, beat the cream cheese on medium until smooth. Turn the mixer to low and add the heavy cream in a slow steady stream, mixing until combined. Increase the speed to medium-high and whisk until stiff peaks form, 3 to 4 minutes.

Add half the whipped cream mixture to the sweetened condensed milk mixture and whisk until completely combined. Using a rubber spatula, gently fold the remaining whipped cream mixture until no streaks remain. Add the chopped chocolate and mix to combine. Pour into a 9-inch loaf pan or Pullman pan with a lid and freeze until firm, 6 hours or, covered, up to 1 week.

BLOOD ORANGE NO-CHURN ICE CREAM

One bite of this ice cream, and my mind immediately goes to humid summer evenings when I was young. My sister, brother, and I would tuck ourselves downstairs in the only corner of our house that was cool. There, stashed in the freezer, was a box of orange Creamsicles ice cream bars, our summer treat of choice. We would eat them slowly, the cold pops helping us momentarily forget the July sun and our friends' air-conditioned homes where sleep came easy. This no-churn re-creation is made with blood oranges, which are slightly more bitter than regular oranges. The bitter note offsets the sweetened condensed milk nicely. This ice cream is delicious all alone or paired with Orange Pie (page 213) or Chocolate Lava Cakes (page 295).

One 14-ounce can (396 g) sweetened condensed milk

½ cup blood orange juice

1 tablespoon pure vanilla extract

1 tablespoon triple sec, or other orange liqueur (optional)

2 teaspoons grated blood orange zest

¼ teaspoon salt

2 ounces (57 g) cream cheese, room temperature

2 cups heavy cream

In a large bowl, whisk the sweetened condensed milk, orange juice, vanilla, triple sec, orange zest, and salt until completely combined.

In the bowl of a stand mixer fitted with a whisk, beat the cream cheese on medium until smooth. Turn the mixer to low and add the heavy cream in a slow steady stream, mixing until combined. Increase the speed to medium-high and whisk until stiff peaks form, 3 to 4 minutes.

Add half the whipped cream mixture to the sweetened condensed milk mixture and whisk until completely combined. Using a rubber spatula, gently fold in the remaining whipped cream mixture until no streaks remain. Pour into a 9-inch loaf pan or Pullman pan with a lid and freeze until firm, 6 hours or, covered, up to 1 week.

COFFEE NO-CHURN ICE CREAM
WITH CACAO NIBS

Coffee is a great ingredient to use in this no-churn ice cream; its bitter flavor is tamed by the milk, but in turn, it helps cut the sweetness. I often pour a shot of hot coffee over the top of this ice cream after it's been scooped into my bowl. I like to serve this with Chocolate Cake with Chocolate Buttercream (page 137) or warm Coffee Blondies (page 258).

One 14-ounce can (396 g) sweetened
  condensed milk

½ cup strong coffee, cold

1 tablespoon pure vanilla extract

2 ounces (57 g) cream cheese, at room
  temperature

2 cups heavy cream

⅓ cup (38 g) cacao nibs

In a large bowl, whisk the sweetened condensed milk, coffee, vanilla, and salt until completely combined.

In the bowl of a stand mixer fitted with a whisk, beat the cream cheese on medium until smooth. Turn the mixer to low and add the heavy cream in a slow steady stream, mixing until combined. Increase the speed to medium-high and whisk until stiff peaks form, 3 to 4 minutes.

Add half the whipped cream mixture to the sweetened condensed milk mixture and whisk until completely combined. Using a rubber spatula, gently fold in the remaining whipped cream mixture until no streaks remain. Stir in the cacao nibs. Pour into a 9-inch loaf pan or Pullman pan with a lid and freeze until firm, 6 hours or, covered, up to 1 week.

PUMPKIN NO-CHURN ICE CREAM

Pumpkin sometimes ends up in odd places (for instance, in my latte), but once autumn arrives and sweaters are part of my everyday attire, that big orange gourd calls to me, promising comfort. Subtle pumpkin flavor, warm spices, and a creamy texture make this no-churn ice cream a perfect treat for the colder months. I like to serve it alongside pumpkin pie, sandwiched between gingersnaps, or just by its lovely little self.

One 14-ounce can (396 g) sweetened condensed milk

¾ cup unsweetened pumpkin puree

1 teaspoon pure vanilla extract

½ teaspoon ground cinnamon

¼ teaspoon ground ginger

⅛ teaspoon grated nutmeg

⅛ teaspoon ground cloves

¼ teaspoon salt

2 ounces (57 g) cream cheese, room temperature

2 cups heavy cream

In a large bowl, whisk the sweetened condensed milk, pumpkin puree, vanilla, cinnamon, ginger, nutmeg, cloves, and salt in a large bowl until completely combined.

In the bowl of a stand mixer fitted with a whisk, beat the cream cheese on medium until smooth. Turn the mixer to low and add the heavy cream in a slow steady stream, mixing until combined. Increase the speed to medium-high and whisk until stiff peaks form, 3 to 4 minutes.

Add half of the whipped cream mixture to the sweetened condensed milk and whisk until completely combined. Using a rubber spatula, gently fold in the remaining whipped cream mixture until no streaks remain. Pour into a 9-inch loaf pan or Pullman pan with a lid and freeze until firm, 6 hours or, covered, up to 1 week.

OLIVE OIL NO-CHURN ICE CREAM
WITH VANILLA BEAN

Olive oil may seem like an odd ingredient to put in ice cream, but it is excellent paired with the sweet milk and vanilla seeds. I love surprising guests with it for dessert and watch their furrowed brows relax after taking one bite, realizing it is, in fact, delicious. This tastes amazing on warm Brownies (page 257) or served alongside Chocolate Cake with Chocolate Buttercream (page 137).

One 14-ounce can (396 g) sweetened condensed milk

½ cup good olive oil

2 teaspoons pure vanilla extract

1 vanilla bean, seeds scraped

¼ teaspoon salt

2 ounces (57 g) cream cheese, room temperature

2 cups heavy cream

In a large bowl, whisk the sweetened condensed milk, olive oil, vanilla, vanilla bean seeds, and salt until completely combined.

In the bowl of a stand mixer fitted with a whisk, beat the cream cheese on medium until smooth. Turn the mixer to low and add the heavy cream in a slow steady stream, mixing until combined. Increase the speed to medium-high and whisk until stiff peaks form, 3 to 4 minutes.

Add half of the whipped cream mixture to the sweetened condensed milk mixture and whisk until completely combined. Using a rubber spatula, gently fold in the remaining whipped cream mixture until no streaks remain. Pour into a 9-inch loaf pan or Pullman pan with a lid and freeze until firm, 6 hours or, covered, up to 1 week.

PEANUT BUTTER NO-CHURN ICE CREAM

I have a terrible weakness for chocolate and peanut butter in any and all forms. I like it in pies, in candy, and in frozen treats alike. This ice cream is incredibly rich, and a little bit goes a very long way. I serve it in small bowls along with Chocolate Magic Shell (page 301) to get my peanut butter and chocolate fix, but it also works well sandwiched between Peanut Butter Cookies (page 241).

One 14-ounce can (396 g) sweetened condensed milk

⅓ cup creamy peanut butter

1 tablespoon pure vanilla extract

¼ teaspoon salt

2 ounces (57 g) cream cheese, at room temperature

2 cups heavy cream

In a large bowl, whisk the sweetened condensed milk, peanut butter, vanilla, and salt until completely combined.

In the bowl of a stand mixer fitted with a whisk, beat the cream cheese on medium until smooth. Turn the mixer to low and add the heavy cream in a slow steady stream, mixing until combined. Increase the speed to medium-high and whisk until stiff peaks form, 3 to 4 minutes.

Add half the whipped cream mixture to the sweetened condensed milk mixture and whisk until completely combined. Using a rubber spatula, gently fold in the remaining whipped cream mixture until no streaks remain. Pour into a 9-inch loaf pan or Pullman pan with a lid and freeze until firm, 6 hours or, covered, up to 1 week.

ICE CREAM SANDWICHES

❦

Ice Cream Sandwiches are basically a more sophisticated version of everyone's favorite childhood classic: cookies and milk. Almost any combination of cookies and ice cream will work here, but I've included a cookie recipe that is soft and tender and complements all of the ice creams in this chapter. *makes 11 to 12 ice cream sandwiches*

1 recipe no-churn ice cream, any flavor

2 cups (288 g) plus 2 tablespoons all-purpose flour

1 teaspoon baking soda

¾ teaspoon salt

½ pound (2 sticks; 227 g) unsalted butter, room temperature

½ cup (99 g) granulated sugar

¾ cup (149 g) packed brown sugar

1 large egg

2 teaspoons pure vanilla extract

Adjust an oven rack to the middle position. Preheat the oven to 350°F. Line two baking sheets with parchment paper.

In a small bowl, whisk the flour, baking soda, and salt. Set aside.

In the bowl of a stand mixer fitted with a paddle, beat the butter on medium until smooth. Add the granulated and brown sugars and beat on medium until light and fluffy, 2 to 3 minutes. Add the egg and vanilla and mix on medium until combined. Add the flour mixture and mix on low until just combined.

Form the dough into 1-ounce (28 g) balls, placing them on the prepared pans. Place 12 cookies on each sheet.

Bake one sheet at a time, 8 to 11 minutes, rotating the pan halfway through, until the sides are set and golden brown, but the center is still slightly underbaked.

Transfer the pan to a wire rack and let the cookies cool completely on the pan before using.

When you are ready to assemble the ice cream sandwiches, take the ice cream out of the freezer and let it soften for a few minutes to make it easier to spread. Spread ¼ cup softened ice cream on the flat side of a cookie. Sandwich the cookies together and freeze until firm, about 1 hour, and serve. Or wrap and freeze for up to 2 weeks.

CONTINUED

chocolate chip ice cream sandwiches · Add 6 ounces (170g) bittersweet chocolate, chopped into bite-size pieces, to the dough after mixing in the flour.

NOTES: Other cookies that will work well for ice cream sandwiches are Peanut Butter Cookies (page 241), Chocolate Sugar Cookies (page 246), and Oatmeal Cookies with White Chocolate and Golden Raisins (page 242).

A melon baller is a great tool for making small ice cream sandwich cookies. If making smaller cookies, you will need to adjust the baking time, and take the cookies out a few minutes earlier.

Another good way to eat ice cream sandwiches is to indulge while the cookies are still warm. Let the cookies cool on the pan for about 5 minutes before making a sandwich with ¼ cup ice cream and 2 warm cookies. Eat and enjoy.

ROSEMARY NO-CHURN ICE CREAM WITH CHOCOLATE LAVA CAKES

A friend gave me this lava cake recipe years ago, and it's been a favorite ever since. The chocolate flavor is deep and dark, and the warm, gooey chocolate center is almost sinful. I've added more chocolate and a little salt to it, but otherwise it's remained close to the original. I like to serve these cakes with ice cream, and ice cream flavored with rosemary is a heavenly pairing. The sweetness of the condensed milk and the intensity of the chocolate balance the sharp herb perfectly.

ROSEMARY ICE CREAM

One 14-ounce can (396 g) sweetened condensed milk

3 sprigs rosemary

¼ teaspoon salt

2 teaspoons pure vanilla extract

2 ounces (57 g) cream cheese, room temperature

2 cups heavy cream

CHOCOLATE LAVA CAKES

6 ounces (170 g) bittersweet chocolate

9 tablespoons (128 g) unsalted butter, cold

3 large eggs

3 large egg yolks

⅓ cup (66 g) sugar

1 teaspoon pure vanilla extract

1 tablespoon bourbon (optional)

¼ teaspoon salt

5 tablespoons (45 g) all-purpose flour

FOR THE ICE CREAM: In a small saucepan over medium-low heat, bring the sweetened condensed milk, rosemary sprigs, and salt to a simmer. Keep an eye on the mixture; the sweetened condensed milk can easily burn. Turn off the heat and let the rosemary steep for 2 hours. Remove the rosemary sprigs and transfer the milk mixture into a large bowl. Stir in the vanilla. Place the bowl in the refrigerator and chill until cool to the touch, about 2 hours.

In the bowl of a stand mixer fitted with a whisk, beat the cream cheese on medium until smooth. Turn the mixer to low and add the heavy cream in a slow steady stream, mixing until combined. Increase the speed to medium-high and whisk until stiff peaks form, 3 to 4 minutes.

Add half the whipped cream mixture to the sweetened condensed milk mixture

CONTINUED

and whisk until completely combined. Using a rubber spatula, gently fold in the remaining whipped cream mixture until no streaks remain. Pour into a 9-inch loaf pan or Pullman pan with a lid and freeze until firm, 6 hours or, covered, up to 1 week.

FOR THE CHOCOLATE LAVA CAKES: Adjust an oven rack to the middle position. Preheat the oven to 375°F.

In a small saucepan over medium-low heat, melt the chocolate and butter, making sure the chocolate is completely melted and smooth. Set aside to cool slightly.

In the bowl of a stand mixer fitted with a paddle, beat the eggs, yolks, and sugar on medium-high until pale yellow and doubled in volume, 5 minutes. Add the vanilla, bourbon (if using), and salt and mix on low to combine. Add the flour and mix on low just until it is incorporated. Add the chocolate and butter and mix gently with a rubber spatula.

Fill 6 ramekins halfway with the batter and place them on a baking sheet. Bake 11 to 12 minutes. The edges should be starting to bake up, but the center should still look underdone.

Transfer the baking sheet to a wire rack. Let the cakes cool a few minutes, before serving with the rosemary ice cream.

VARIATION

basil no-churn ice cream · Substitute ½ cup fresh basil leaves for the rosemary. In a food processor fitted with a steel blade, process the basil, sweetened condensed milk, vanilla, and salt until the basil is finely chopped. Transfer the mixture to a large bowl and fold in the whipped cream as directed.

NOTES: These lava cakes would pair well with any of the ice creams from this chapter, as well as Crème Fraîche (page 305) or Whipped Cream (page 306). They are also delicious on their own.

S'MORES ICE CREAM CAKE

This ice cream cake is on the extravagant side, with layers of graham cracker crumbs, two kinds of ice cream, and a toasty meringue top. I like to serve it in very thin pieces, as less is more for this dessert. It's a showstopper for sure, perfect for summer birthday parties and special events. *serves 6 to 8*

1 recipe Vanilla No-Churn Ice Cream (page 277)

1 recipe Chocolate No-Churn Ice Cream (page 278)

1½ cups (150 g) graham cracker crumbs

2 tablespoons sugar

5 tablespoons (72 g) unsalted butter, melted and cooled

5 large egg whites

1 cup (198 g) sugar

¼ teaspoon salt

2 teaspoons pure vanilla extract

Adjust an oven rack to the middle position. Preheat the oven to 325°F. Line a baking sheet with parchment paper and line a Pullman pan with a parchment sling (page 15). (You can also use a 9-inch loaf pan, but you will need to use less ice cream.)

In a medium bowl stir the graham cracker crumbs and sugar to combine. Add the melted butter and stir until evenly coated. Transfer the crumbs to the prepared baking sheet and spread them evenly across the parchment paper. Bake 8 to 10 minutes, until the crumbs are golden brown and fragrant.

Transfer the pan to a wire rack and let cool completely.

Use a measuring cup or spoon to press 1 cup (100 g) cooled crumbs evenly on bottom of the prepared Pullman pan or loaf pan. Top with the Vanilla Ice Cream, pressing it into an even layer. Sprinkle the remaining crumbs evenly over the ice cream and top with the Chocolate Ice Cream. Place the ice cream cake in the freezer and freeze for at least 6 hours or overnight before topping with meringue.

FOR THE MERINGUE TOPPING: Put about an inch of water in a medium saucepan and bring it to a gentle boil.

In the bowl of a stand mixer, stir the egg whites, sugar, and salt to combine. Place the bowl over the saucepan, being careful not to let the water touch the bottom of the bowl. Stir with a rubber spatula until the sugar is completely melted and reaches a temperature of 160°F, 4 to 5 minutes. While you are stirring, be sure to scrape down

CONTINUED

the sides of the bowl with the spatula—this will ensure no sugar grains are lurking on the sides and also help prevent the egg whites from cooking.

Remove the bowl from the heat and place it in the stand mixer fitted with a whisk. Whisk on medium-high until stiff, glossy peaks form, 8 to 10 minutes. The bowl should have cooled down to room temperature at this point. Add the vanilla and beat until combined.

Use the parchment sling to gently remove the cake from the loaf pan. Working quickly, remove the parchment paper and set the loaf cake on a serving platter.

Use a spatula to spread the meringue evenly over the top of the ice cream cake and, if desired, use a spoon to create curls. Hold a kitchen blowtorch 1 or 2 inches away from the cake and touch the flame down in between the curls. The curls will toast and brown (if the curls set on fire, you can blow them out). Slice the cake and serve immediately.

CHOCOLATE MAGIC SHELL

Just as its name states, this little recipe is magic. When the warm chocolate topping hits cold, creamy ice cream, it hardens almost instantly, creating a crunchy shell that is downright delicious. This sorcery will work on any of the ice creams in this chapter, but I especially love it with Peanut Butter No-Churn Ice Cream (page 291), Pumpkin No-Churn Ice Cream (page 287), and Vanilla No-Churn Ice Cream (page 277).

1 cup (170 g) semisweet or
    bittersweet chocolate chips
¼ cup refined coconut oil

1 teaspoon pure vanilla extract
Pinch salt

Place the chocolate, coconut oil, vanilla, and salt in a large liquid measuring cup or other microwave-safe dish. Microwave on high 30 seconds. Stir. Repeat until the mixture is melted and completely smooth. Let cool slightly and then pour over ice cream.

The magic shell will keep for several months and can be stored at room temperature. It may separate over time, so give it a stir before using. If the magic shell hardens, you can gently reheat it in the microwave.

VARIATION

white chocolate magic shell · Replace the semisweet chocolate chips with white chocolate chips.

NOTE: Extra-virgin coconut oil does not work as well here because it will make the magic shell taste like coconut. Refined coconut oil has a more subtle flavor.

chapter seven

HOMEMADE STAPLES

Store-bought condiments and staples are perfectly fine, but sometimes it's nice to make them from scratch. The items in this chapter are used in recipes throughout the book, and I make all of them frequently in my own kitchen. Crème Fraîche (page 305) is one I like to have on hand at all times, and Vanilla Extract (page 307) is a fun project that is also cost-effective. Many of these items also make great gifts; the Flavored Sugars (page 308) can be placed in decorative jars and given away, and the Caramel Sauce (page 316) would be lovely to bring to a neighbor or a housewarming party.

CRÈME FRAÎCHE

Barron's *Food Lover's Companion* defines crème fraîche (pronounced krehm FRESH) as a "matured, thickened cream [with] a slightly tangy, nutty flavor and velvety rich texture." My own personal definition is creamy, dreamy loveliness that tastes good on pretty much everything. Crème fraiche is similar to sour cream, but is less sour and often has a higher percentage of butterfat. It also endures heat much better than sour cream and doesn't break when introduced to high temperatures. It can be used in sweet and savory applications. Look for it in Crème Fraîche Scones (page 41) and use it to accompany Mixed Berry Galettes (page 223) and Blackberry-Apricot Hand Pies (page 227). *makes about 4 cups*

> 3 cups heavy cream
> ¾ cup buttermilk

In a large bowl, whisk the cream and buttermilk. Cover the top of the bowl with several individual layers of cheesecloth; I usually cover it with four layers. Place a rubber band or tie a string around the bowl to keep the cheesecloth in place. Let the bowl sit out at room tememperature for 24 hours and up to 3 days, until it has thickened. The time depends on the outside temperature both outside and in your home. The buttermilk contains active cultures ("good" bacteria) that prevent the cream from spoiling and is acidic enough to deter "bad" bacteria from growing.

When it is thickened and ready to use, gently stir and transfer the mixture to an airtight container and refrigerate. It can be refrigerated up to 1 week.

NOTES: Covering the crème fraîche with cheesecloth helps keep dust and bugs out, while still picking up bacteria in the air, which can flavor the crème fraîche and give it a unique taste. If you prefer, you can make the crème fraîche in a large covered jar. Pour the heavy cream and buttermilk in the jar, seal it tightly, and shake well. Let it sit at room temperature for 24 to 48 hours. Transfer to the refrigerator once it's thick and ready to use.

The buttermilk can be replaced with sour cream or whole milk plain yogurt, as long as it contains active cultures.

WHIPPED CREAM

Homemade whipped cream is so delicious and really simple to make. I've included a few variations because flavored cream can be quite a treat and a good way to add a spin on a recipe. I always serve whipped cream with Straight-Up Apple Pie (page 195) and Cherry-Rhubarb Crisp with White Wine (page 217), but of course, it goes with everything in the "Pies and Tarts" chapter. *makes about 3 cups*

1½ cups heavy cream, chilled
2 tablespoons sugar

½ teaspoon pure vanilla extract
Pinch salt

At least 10 minutes before whipping the cream, place the mixer bowl and whisk in the freezer and let chill. In a stand mixer fitted with the chilled whisk, whisk the heavy cream, sugar, and vanilla in the chilled bowl on low for 30 to 45 seconds. Increase the speed to medium and beat 30 to 45 seconds. Increase the speed to high and beat until cream is smooth, thick, and nearly double in volume, 30 to 60 seconds. The whipped cream can be made 2 hours ahead of time and stored in the refrigerator.

VARIATIONS

vanilla bean whipped cream · Add the seeds of one vanilla bean pod to the cream, along with the sugar, vanilla, and salt.

lemon whipped cream · Add 1 tablespoon lemon juice and 1 teaspoon grated lemon zest along with the sugar, vanilla, and salt.

chocolate whipped cream · Add 3 ounces (85 g) bittersweet chocolate, melted and cooled, along with the sugar, vanilla, and salt.

cream cheese whipped cream · Add 2 ounces (57 g) cream cheese, at room temperature, to the chilled bowl, before the other ingredients are added. Beat the cream cheese on medium until smooth. Add the sugar, vanilla, and salt and beat on medium until smooth. With the mixer running on low, add the heavy cream in a slow, steady stream and whisk until combined. Increase to medium-high and beat until smooth, thick, and nearly double in volume.

VANILLA EXTRACT

I started making my own vanilla extract a few years back, both because it tastes delicious and because it ends up being much cheaper than the store-bought bottles. This vanilla extract can be used in any of the recipes in this book. Vanilla beans can be purchased online in bulk, see "Resources" (page 321).

6 vanilla beans

1 cup vodka (bourbon, rum, or brandy can also be used here; vodka will have the lightest, cleanest flavor)

Use a knife to split the vanilla beans in half lengthwise, leaving about ½ inch at each end intact. Put the vanilla beans in a glass bottle or jar (a large mason jar works well) and cover with vodka (or other alcohol). Tightly close the bottle and store in a cool, dry place, away from the light for at least 8 weeks. I like to age my vanilla for an entire year, but if you can't wait that long, anytime after 8 weeks will do. Give the bottle a shake every week or so. The vanilla can be strained if desired, but leaving the seeds and pods in the jar will not hurt the vanilla, and only add to the flavor. This recipe can easily be doubled or tripled.

FLAVORED SUGARS

Flavored sugars are nice to have around and can add unique flavor to your baked goods. I use them quite often in my kitchen. I like to sprinkle cardamom sugar on the Crème Fraîche Scones (page 41) just before baking, and the lavender sugar is delicious dusted on the Berry Cream Pie (page 206). I also occasionally sprinkle whatever flavored sugar I have around in my coffee or tea. Store the sugars in a cool, dark place. Flavored sugars will last for 2 weeks.

CINNAMON SUGAR

1 cup (198 g) sugar

1 tablespoon cinnamon

Place the sugar and cinnamon in a jar, seal the lid, and shake to combine.

CARDAMOM SUGAR

1 cup (198 g) sugar

1 tablespoon ground cardamom

Place the sugar and ground cardamom in a jar. Seal the lid and shake to combine.

LEMON SUGAR

1 cup sugar

Grated zest of 1 lemon

Place the sugar and lemon zest in the bowl of a food processor fitted with a steel blade. Pulse until zest is broken down into the sugar, 6 or 7 times. Transfer to a jar and seal.

PUMPKIN PIE SUGAR

1 cup (198 g) sugar

1 teaspoon ground cinnamon

½ teaspoon ground ginger

½ teaspoon grated nutmeg

¼ teaspoon ground cloves

Place the sugar, cinnamon, ginger, nutmeg, and cloves in a jar. Seal the lid and shake to combine.

VANILLA BEAN SUGAR

1 cup (198 g) sugar

1 vanilla bean, seeds scraped and
  pod reserved

Place the sugar, vanilla bean seeds, and the pod in a jar. Seal the lid and shake to combine.

CACAO NIB SUGAR

1 cup (198 g) sugar

2 tablespoons cacao nibs

Place the sugar and cacao nibs in the bowl of a food processor fitted with a steel blade. Pulse until the cacao nibs are broken down into tiny pieces in the sugar, 6 or 7 times. Transfer to a jar and seal.

LAVENDER SUGAR

1 cup (198 g) sugar

2 tablespoons culinary lavender

Place the sugar and lavender in a food processor fitted with a steel blade and process until the leaves are chopped so small they look like green crystals in the sugar. Transfer to a jar and seal.

CHOCOLATE GANACHE

Chocolate ganache is rich and intense and used in a variety of applications. In this book I pair it with Chocolate Cheesecake (page 172), but it could also be used on the (Almost) No-Bake Cheesecake (page 175), or spooned over ice cream.

6 ounces (170 g) bittersweet chocolate, chopped fine

¾ cup heavy cream

½ teaspoon pure vanilla extract

Pinch salt

Place the chocolate in a small bowl. Heat the heavy cream in a small saucepan until it is simmering and just about to boil. Pour the cream over the chocolate, cover the bowl with plastic wrap, and let sit for 5 minutes.

Remove the plastic and whisk until completely smooth. Add the vanilla and salt and whisk to combine. Cool to room temperature before using.

PASTRY CREAM

The first time I made pastry cream, I was working with Zoë François on a chaotic but incredibly fun photoshoot. I was back in the kitchen baking loaves of bread and brioche, trying to stay ahead of schedule and have everything ready for the next photo. Pastry cream was needed, and I pretended I knew what I was doing when Zoë handed me the recipe and told me to make it quick. Somehow I pulled it off—there before me in the pan was a thick, yellow custard. I took the pan off the heat to show her how pretty it was. She took it from my hands and placed it back on the stovetop. "Cook out the starch!" she insisted. "Whisk it until it's glossy and smooth, or you'll have a grainy mess." I meekly obeyed and ended up with the most beautiful, smooth pastry cream. Making pastry cream now, I always remember her directions. Cooking the custard for a few extra minutes helps cook out the starch and keeps the cream from separating.

These days, I start my pastry cream in a stand mixer, beating the eggs and sugar until thick and pale, then slowly add warm milk and cream to temper the eggs. It is a little more hands off and less messy than the way I used to make pastry cream. *makes 2 cups*

7 large egg yolks

1¼ cups (248 g) sugar

¼ teaspoon salt

1 vanilla bean, seeds scraped

¼ cup (28 g) cornstarch

1 cup whole milk

1 cup heavy cream

1 tablespoon (15 g) unsalted butter, cold

2 teaspoons pure vanilla extract

In the bowl of a stand mixer fitted with a paddle, beat the egg yolks, sugar, salt, and vanilla bean seeds on medium-high until very thick and pale yellow, about 5 minutes. Scrape down the sides of the bowl and add the cornstarch. Turn the mixer to low and mix until combined.

In a small saucepan over medium-low heat, heat the milk and heavy cream until just scalded. Remove from the heat and pour into a medium measuring cup with a pourable spout.

With the mixer running on low, very slowly add the hot milk mixture. Mix until completely combined.

Transfer to a medium heavy-bottomed saucepan and add the vanilla bean pod. Cook over low heat, stirring constantly with a wooden spoon, until the pastry cream becomes very thick and begins to boil, 5 to 7 minutes. Whisk the mixture, until the pastry cream thickens, similar to a pudding, and is glossy and smooth, 3 to 4 minutes. Remove from the heat, strain the pastry cream through a sieve into a medium bowl, and discard the vanilla bean pod. Stir in the butter and vanilla. Cover with plastic wrap, making sure the wrap sits directly on top of the cream (this will help keep it from forming a skin). Place the bowl in the freezer for 15 minutes, then transfer to the refrigerator until well chilled.

VARIATION

chocolate pastry cream · Add 6 ounces (170 g) melted bittersweet chocolate to the saucepan just before straining the pastry cream. Whisk until fully incorporated, and strain the pastry cream as directed.

crème mousseline · Also known as German buttercream, crème mousseline is a pastry cream buttercream. If you have leftover pastry cream, you can add room temperature butter to it, whip it in your stand mixer, and use it to frost cakes. It is wonderful with the Chocolate Cake (page 129). Use 1 cup (227 g) unsalted butter to 2 cups (454 g) pastry cream.

CONFECTIONERS' SUGAR GLAZE

1½ cups (170 g) confectioners' sugar

2 to 4 tablespoons whole milk

½ teaspoon pure vanilla extract

Pinch salt

In a medium bowl, whisk together the confectioners' sugar, 2 tablespoons milk, vanilla, and salt. Add more milk, 1 tablespoon at a time, to thin the icing to a preferred consistency. For a pure white icing, omit the vanilla.

STREUSEL

I use streusel on Berry Muffins with Streusel (page 86) and Butterscotch Crumble (page 231), but it also works well on bars, scones, coffeecakes, and tarts. Often I'll make a large batch of this and keep it in the fridge; it keeps for 3 to 4 days chilled and for 1 month frozen. This recipe can easily be doubled. *makes 2 cups*

⅔ cup (96 g) all-purpose flour

⅓ cup (66 g) granulated sugar

⅓ cup (66 g) packed brown sugar

½ cup (50 g) almond flour, chopped pecans, or oats

¼ teaspoon salt

¼ teaspoon ground cinnamon

6 tablespoons (86 g) unsalted butter, room temperature, cut into 6 pieces

In the bowl of a stand mixer, combine the all-purpose flour, granulated and brown sugars, almond flour, salt, and cinnamon on low. With the mixer on low, add the butter, 1 tablespoon at a time, until the mixture comes together but still is quite crumbly.

BROWN BUTTER

{beurre noisette}

Browning butter is a great kitchen technique to know; it enhances the flavor of the butter in both savory and sweet applications. It's not difficult to make; all you need is some butter, a skillet, and a watchful eye.

Unsalted butter, cold

Melt the butter in a light-colored, heavy-bottomed skillet or saucepan over medium-low heat. Swirl the butter around with a rubber spatula as it melts and starts to bubble. When it starts bubbling, increase the heat to medium and keep stirring the butter until it boils and begins to foam, 3 to 5 minutes. It will smell nutty and you'll start to see little brown bits on the bottom of the pan. Keep stirring, making sure to gently scrape the bottom of the pan with the spatula as you do so. At this point, the butter will begin to quickly change from light brown to dark to burned, so keep a close eye on the pan. I like to take the butter to a dark golden brown for lots of flavor. Once it is golden brown, remove from the heat, and pour the butter and any bits or flecks on the bottom of the pan into a heatproof bowl. The browned butter can be used immediately or cooled to room temperature and stored in the refrigerator for later use (see Brown Butter Buttercream, page 161).

NOTES: Butter is made up of milk fat, water, and milk solids. As the butter is heated, the water evaporates, and the milk solids are left behind in the hot pan, along with the milk fat. The solids begin to brown and toast as they continue to heat.

Because the water evaporates when the butter boils, you won't be left with as much butter as you started with. In some applications this can be an issue. If you are substituting brown butter in a recipe that calls for regular butter, you will want to brown more butter than the recipe calls for, then weigh the butter to get the correct amount for the recipe.

Using a light-colored skillet will help you easily tell when the butter has changed from light to dark brown. A dark skillet often can result in burned brown butter.

The size of skillet or pot to use depends on how much butter you are browning. If you are browning a little butter, use a medium skillet. For a lot of butter, use a large skillet. I use a traditional skillet to brown my butter, but a nonstick skillet will also work.

SOUR CHERRY SAUCE

Sour cherries just might be the best part of the summer, and I look for any opportunity to get my hands on them. This sauce is on the tart side, mouth-puckering in the best possible way. It pairs perfectly with Classic Cheesecake (page 168), but also is divine spilled warm over Vanilla No-Churn Ice Cream (page 277). *makes 2 cups*

12 ounces (341 g) pitted sour cherries

¼ cup (50 g) sugar

1 tablespoon cornstarch

Pinch of salt

Pinch of ground cinnamon

Vanilla bean, seeds scraped

1 tablespoon kirsch (optional)

In a medium saucepan over medium heat, cook the cherries, sugar, cornstarch, salt, cinnamon, and vanilla bean seeds, and vanilla bean pod until the cherries release their juices and the mixture turns glossy and thick, 5 to 7 minutes. A wooden spoon dragged across the bottom of the pan should leave a streak. Remove from the heat and add the kirsch (if using), stirring gently to combine. Remove the vanilla bean pod before serving.

COFFEE SYRUP

This recipe came about by accident. I was making a coffee soak for a cake, and halfway through boiling the sugar and coffee I realized I'd like to see this on my pancakes as well. I make a double batch whenever company is coming over, as it's been received quite well by family and friends alike. Pair with the Dutch Baby (page 48), or whenever you'd normally use maple syrup. *makes about 1½ cups*

2 cups strong coffee, room temperature

2 cups (396 g) sugar

1 teaspoon salt

2 tablespoons (29 g) unsalted butter

1 teaspoon pure vanilla extract

2 tablespoons Frangelico (optional)

In a medium saucepan over medium-high heat, bring the coffee, sugar, and salt to a boil. Continue to boil until reduced to 1½ cups, 10 to 12 minutes.

Remove from the heat and add the butter, vanilla, and Frangelico (if using); stir to combine. Let cool 10 minutes before serving. Can be stored in the refrigerator for 1 week.

CARAMEL SAUCE

Homemade caramel sauce may need your utmost attention while bubbling and boiling, but it is worth taking the time to make. This sauce works well with any ice cream in this book, but I especially like it paired with the Pumpkin No-Churn Ice Cream (page 287). *makes 1½ cups*

¼ cup water, room temperature

1¼ cups (248 g) sugar

½ teaspoon salt

8 tablespoons (1 stick; 113 g) unsalted butter, cold, cut into 8 pieces

½ cup heavy cream

1 tablespoon pure vanilla extract

Have all your ingredients set up near the stove, ready to go.

Pour the water in a medium, heavy-bottomed saucepan (the caramel will bubble up quite a bit once it starts cooking, so it's important to have a pan that is deep and also has a heavy bottom to prevent burning). Sprinkle the sugar and salt on top. Very gently stir the ingredients together, just until the sugar is completely wet, being careful not to get the water or sugar on the sides of the pan. Cook over medium heat, shaking the pan occasionally to stir the sugar while it melts. When the sugar crystals have completely dissolved, increase the heat to medium-high. The sugar will begin to foam. Let it bubble and boil 3 to 5 minutes, keeping an eye on it so it doesn't boil over. Give the pan a swirl every once in a while to help the sugar turn color evenly. The sugar will begin to turn dark golden brown at this point, and you want to keep it bubbling until it just begins to smoke. Remove from the heat and add the butter, whisking carefully (remember, the sugar is crazy hot). Whisk in the heavy cream, followed by the vanilla. Set the caramel aside until ready to use.

VARIATION

burnt honey caramel · Instead of using 1¼ cups (248 g) sugar, substitute 1 cup (198 g) sugar and ½ cup (168 g) honey.

salty caramel · When you take the caramel off the heat, add ½ teaspoon fleur de sel.

toasted sesame caramel · Add 3 tablespoons toasted sesame oil along with the vanilla.

CONVERSIONS

All conversions have been rounded up or down to the nearest whole number.

WEIGHT CONVERSION

½ ounce = 14 grams

1 ounce = 28 grams

1½ ounces = 43 grams

2 ounces = 57 grams

2½ ounces = 71 grams

3 ounces = 85 grams

3½ ounces = 99 grams

4 ounces = 113 grams

4½ ounces = 128 grams

5 ounces = 142 grams

8 ounces = 227 grams

10 ounces = 283 grams

12 ounces = 340 grams

16 ounces = 454 grams

OVEN TEMPERATURES

300°F = 150°C

350°F = 180°C

375°F = 190°C

400°F = 200°C

425°F = 220°C

450°F = 230°C

VOLUME EQUIVALENTS

TEASPOONS TO ML

⅛ teaspoon	0.5 mL
¼ teaspoon	1 mL
½ teaspoon	2 mL
¾ teaspoon	4 mL
1 teaspoon	5 mL
1¼ teaspoons	6 mL
1½ teaspoons	7 mL
1¾ teaspoons	9 mL
2 teaspoons	10 mL
2½ teaspoons	12 mL
2¾ teaspoons	14 mL
4 teaspoons	20 mL
4½ teaspoons	22 mL

TABLESPOONS TO ML

1 tablespoon	15 mL
2 tablespoons	30 mL
3 tablespoons	45 mL
5 tablespoons	75 mL
6 tablespoons	90 mL

CUPS TO ML

¼ cup	60 mL
⅓ cup	75 mL
½ cup	125 mL
⅔ cup	150 mL
¾ cup	175 mL
1 cup	250 mL
1¼ cups	300 mL
1⅓ cups	325 mL
1½ cups	375 mL
1⅔ cups	400 mL
1¾ cups	425 mL
2 cups	500 mL
2¼ cups	550 mL
2⅓ cups	575 mL
2½ cups	625 mL
2⅔ cups	650 mL
2¾ cups	675 mL
3 cups	750 mL
3⅓ cups	825 mL
3½ cups	875 mL
3⅔ cups	900 mL
3¾ cups	925 mL
4 cups	1 L
4½ cups	1.1 L
5 cups	1.25 L
6 cups	1.5 L
8 cups	2 L

CONVERSIONS FOR COMMONLY USED INGREDIENTS

1 cup all-purpose flour = 5 ounces = 142 grams

1 cup whole wheat flour = 5.5 ounces = 156 grams

1 cup granulated sugar = 7 ounces = 198 grams

1 cup packed brown sugar = 7 ounces = 198 grams

1 cup confectioners' sugar = 4 ounces = 113 grams

1 cup cocoa powder = 3.5 ounces = 100 grams

8 tablespoons butter (1 stick) = 4 ounces = 113 grams

16 tablespoons butter (2 sticks) = 8 ounces = 227 grams

BIBLIOGRAPHY

My baking training came from a variety of sources. Much of it was hands-on in the workplace, guided by Larry and Colleen Wolner, but over the years other bakers and books have helped teach and shape my knowledge. Zoë François is another mentor on my journey, and her help has been invaluable. Many ideas, techniques, and recipe evolutions were picked up here and there over the years, and it would be impossible to site all of them. However, I want to highlight a few books that have been well-loved in my library and have given me so much helpful information or inspired a starting point for a recipe.

Rose Levy Beranbaum, *The Pie and Pastry Bible*. New York: Scribner, 1998.

Flo Braker, *The Simple Art of Perfect Baking*. San Francisco: Chronicle Books, 1985.

Beth Dooley and Lucia Watson, *Savoring the Seasons of the Northern Heartland*. New York: Alfred A. Knopf, 1994.

Editors at America's Test Kitchen, *Cook's Illustrated Baking Book*. Brookline, MA: America's Test Kitchen, 2013.

M. F. K. Fisher, *The Art of Eating*. Hoboken, NJ: Wiley Publishing, Inc., 1937.

Ina Garten, *The Barefoot Contessa*. New York: Clarkson Potter, 1999.

Darra Goldstein, *Sugar and Sweets*. New York: Oxford, 2015.

Sharon Tyler Herbst and Ron Herbst, *Food Lover's Companion*. Hauppauge, NY: Barron's Educational Series, 2007.

Jeff Hertzberg and Zoë François, *The New Artisan Bread in Five Minutes a Day*. New York: St. Martin's Press, 2013.

Nigella Lawson, *How to Be a Domestic Goddess*. New York: Hyperion, 2001.

Sarabeth Levine, *Sarabeth's Bakery from My Kitchen to Yours*. New York: Rizzoli, 2010.

Matt Lewis and Renato Poliafito, *Baked Explorations*. New York: Stewart, Tabori & Chang, 2010.

Martha Stewart Living Omnimedia, *Martha Stewart's Baking Handbook*. New York: Clarkson Potter, 2005.

Alice Medrich, *Bittersweet*. New York: Artisan, 2003.

Moosewood Collective, *Moosewood Restaurant New Classics*. New York: Clarkson Potter, 2001.

Tara O'Brady, *Seven Spoons*. Berkeley: Ten Speed Press, 2015.

Gayle and Joe Ortiz, with Louisa Beers, *The Village Baker*. Berkeley: Ten Speed Press, 1997.

Karen Page and Andrew Dornenburg, *The Flavor Bible*. New York: Little, Brown and Company, 2008.

Kamran Siddiqi, *Hand Made Baking*. San Francisco: Chronicle Books, 2014.

Nigel Slater, *Ripe*. Berkeley: Ten Speed Press, 2010.

Alice Waters, *Chez Panisse Fruit*. New York: HarperCollins, New York, 2002.

HELPFUL WEBSITES

Online sites have been helpful in my baking journey as well. If I have a baking question, I often look to one of these resources for help.

americastestkitchen.com

kingarthurflour.com

seriouseats.com

food52.com

thekitchn.com

zoebakes.com

MUSIC TO BAKE TO

After working in coffee shops for so many years, I got accustomed to baking with background music. I have to admit I was a little obsessive about what music was played when I worked; I always felt it was important to create an atmosphere that was relaxing and engaging to both the customer and the employees, and spent way too many hours creating mix tapes, and then CDs, and then playlists, to play at the shop. While we did listen to all kinds of music and genres, I found myself always coming back to these albums. They have been played so many times in my shops and in my own home, even my kids sing along now.

MORNING TUNES

Nat King Cole · *The Essentials*

Miles Davis · *Bye Bye Blackbird*

Blossom Dearie · *Self-Titled*

Ella Fitzgerald · *Mack the Knife*

Ella Fitzgerald and Louis Armstrong · *Ella and Louis*

Melody Gardot · *My One and Only Thrill*

Stan Getz and João Astrud Gilberto · *Corcovado*

Peggy Lee · *Trav'lin' Light*

Joni Mitchell · *Ladies of the Canyon*

Over the Rhine · *Good Dog, Bad Dog*

The Innocence Mission · *Befriended*

Nick Drake · *Pink Moon*

NIGHT GROOVES

Chet Baker Quartet · *Jazz in Paris Vol 53*

Nicola Conte · *Bossa Per Due*

The Miles Davis Quintet · *Just Relaxin'*

St. Germain · *Tourist*

Saint-Germain Café · *Volume 1*

Koop · *Waltz for Koop*

Feist · *Let It Die*

Bebel Gilberto · *Tanto Tempo*

RESOURCES

EMILE HENRY
emilehenryusa.com
Ceramic cookware

**FORAGE MODERN
WORKSHOP**
foragemodernworkshop.com
Unique tableware

HOPE CREAMERY
hopecreamery.com
The most delicious butter

BEANILLA
beanilla.com
Vanilla beans

KING ARTHUR FLOUR
kingarthurflour.com
Flours, kitchen tools,
equipment, fancy sprinkles,
and other specialty baking
ingredients

LE CREUSET
lecreuset.com
Baking and cooking
equipment

PENZEYS SPICES
penzeys.com
Spices and vanilla beans

SUR LA TABLE
surlatable.com
Baking and cooking tools
and equipment

VALRHONA
valrhona-chocolate.com
Chocolate and cocoa powder

WILLIAMS-SONOMA
williams-sonoma.com
Bakeware, baking utensils,
cake decorating tools

ACKNOWLEDGMENTS

Even as I sit down to type these words of thanks, this whole project still seems like a dream. I spent all of middle school and parts of high school writing short stories, novellas, and poems in the free time I had, dreaming that maybe one day my work would make its way to book form. So while *cookbook* was never in my early plans, I am still pinching myself that here I am, years later, publishing this book.

First, so much thanks to Avery Books and Penguin Canada.

I am grateful for the opportunity to work with my amazing editor, Lucia Watson. Knowing that each phone conversation and email sent is listened to and thoughtfully considered is incredible. I feel so lucky to have my book in such good hands. Thanks also to Andrea Magyar for sending me that most amazing email and making my dream a reality.

Thanks to my literary agent, Jane Dystel, who has taken such good care of me along the way. I appreciate your help and guidance.

Thanks to Forage Modern Workshop, William-Sonoma, Le Creuset, Sur La Table, and Emile Henry for providing marble slabs, serving pieces, and baking equipment for the book.

To all my many recipe testers: First and foremost, the Blue Heron bakers: Diane Leutgeb-Munson, Melanie Murray, and Walker Edwards-Robeson, who baked their way through so much of this book. Thank you, thank you. Zoë François, Joy Summers, Heather Meyen, Yossy Afari, Molly Yeh, Melissa Coleman, Sara Forte, Tara O'Brady, Linda Mueller, Lisa Heaner, Nik Sharma, Billy Green, Alana Kysar, Kate Selner, Jenn Tudor, Jennifer Graham, Kate Watson, Scott Beck, Kristin Zoellner, Prerna Singh, Trish Laughbaum, Diane Atneosen, Linda Heikenene, Amy Wyland, Kristin Zoellner, Ellen Kaldor, and Rebecca Aguilar, your input was invaluable and I appreciate your time and effort spent. Last, Kelsey Tenney, who swooped in at the last minute and baked an incredible amount of recipes in record time. You were a lifesaver.

To Yossy Afari, Ashley Rodriguez, Tara O'Brady, Jeanine Donofrio, and Aimée Wimbush-Bourque, thank you for answering questions, helpful advice, and words of encouragement. I appreciate all your answers to frantic texts and panic-stricken emails.

To Melissa Coleman, for all your help with detail and design, answering frantic texts, and always being so encouraging. I'm so glad we're (kind of) neighbors.

To Jeff Hertzberg and Zoë François for being such great people to work for. I feel like this book might not be here if it wasn't for your taking a chance on me a few years ago and including me on your team. I appreciate all your help and guidance. Thanks also for epic photoshoots and business team lunches. And to Zoë, for all your help in so many ways: talking me through recipes, photos, book covers, and life. I'm so thankful for all our coffee chats and terrible jokes.

To Melody Heide, for your helpful suggestions and writing guidance. I hope one day to be as good a writer as you.

To Bordertown Coffee, for giving me a chance in that teeny-tiny kitchen. I learned so much about baking in my three years working there.

To Larry and Colleen Wolner, every baking compliment I have received, every successful attempt in the kitchen has its roots in the Blue Heron. You both mean so much to me, and I'm so thankful for you.

To Bill Kieffer, for being here for us and being such an amazing help. You're the best kind of Grandpa-neighbor we could have.

To Linda and Jeff Mueller, thank you for your encouragement, for coming our way so often and helping us out, and for always making us laugh. We love you so much.

Angie, Dave, Daniel, Cassie, BJ, and Livvy, I couldn't ask for better siblings and sibling-in-laws. Thank you for all your recipe sampling, kind words, and encouragement throughout the years. You all make my life so much better.

Mom and Dad, I can't thank you enough for always believing in me, and supporting me. You taught me that hard work really does pay off. I am grateful to belong to you.

Winter and River, you are the loveliest little souls, and I'm so glad you're mine. I look forward to all our kitchen adventures.

Adam, your belief in me and respect for what I do both personally and professionally gives me the courage to pursue what I love, including baking my life away. This book wouldn't be here without you. You're my favorite one.

INDEX